SAY
GOODBYE
to
PLASTIC

A SURVIVAL GUIDE FOR PLASTIC-FREE LIVING

SANDRA ANN HARRIS
FOUNDER OF ECOLUNCHBOX

FOREWORD BY DIANNA COHEN
PLASTIC POLLUTION COALITION

SAY GOODBYE TO PLASTIC

Text Copyright © 2020 Sandra Ann Harris

Library of Congress Cataloging-in-Publication Data is available.

ISBN: 978-1-57826-860-3

ECOlunchbox is a member of the California Green Business Network and is a Certified B Corporation™

Book design by Carolyn Kasper

10 9 8 7 6 5 4 3 2 1

Printed in the United States

Contents

Foreword

Never underestimate the power of one individual to create the change the planet needs, all while inspiring others around them to positively contribute to the plastic-free movement. Starting with one small thing, such as a commitment to bring a reusable cup, bottle or bag daily, sets in motion system shifts, behavior change and inspires others.

Saying goodbye to single-use plastic and making a commitment to think "reusable, not disposable" are the first two steps we all can take.

Sandra is one of these individuals. In her inspirational book *Say Goodbye To Plastic*, she tells the story of how she got started in the plastic pollution movement more than a decade ago, providing a straightforward how-to guide for plastic-free living...with good news! We can save money, reduce exposure to toxic chemicals for ourselves, our family and our schools, and communities, and all while we protect the ocean, our waterways and lakes, and air and water from plastic particulate pollution.

It is urgent that we realize how our dependence on and use of plastic pollutes us, our planet and every ecosystem on it. In particular, plastic pollutes and poisons fenceline and frontline communities, seriously impacting communities of color and indigenous communities around the world. Plastic pollutes us at every stage; starting from the extraction of this petroleum-based resource, throughout its manufacturing, during its use, and at end of its life—where it's rarely recycled and more often gets burned or buried—plastic pollutes us all.

In 2009, when we founded Plastic Pollution Coalition and Sandra's plastic-free company ECOlunchbox had just come to market, the world referred to this material as marine debris, litter, rubbish, waste, and garbage. But see how far we have come? If 70-90 percent of marine debris is plastic, then we call it what it is: *plastic*! And when it is getting into the environment and our oceans, air and drinking water... it's plastic pollution. The Plastic Pollution Coalition is made up of more than 1,200 organizations and businesses, including ECOlunchbox, from 77 countries around the world, all working to stop plastic pollution and to raise awareness about plastic's toxic impact on human health, animal health, the ocean and waterways, and the environment.

On the bright side, Sandra reminds us that the power to create change through small acts and behaviors can create a stunning ripple effect. Born on her kitchen table and grown for more than 10 years since, Sandra's company ECOlunchbox has sold hundreds of thousands of plastic-free food containers that have empowered her user community to avert tens of millions of pieces of trash every year. During this same time, by working collaboratively with allies young and old across boundaries and borders, our coalition has ushered in tremendous positive changes in behavior, extended producer responsibility (EPR) policies for businesses, and major reductions and bans on single-use plastics in policy and legislation.

Say Goodbye To Plastic shows us how to break up with plastic now...room by room, task by task. It's easy. We *can* do this, all of us together. Plastic pollutes. Refuse it, don't use it.

—Dianna Cohen,
  CEO & Co-Founder
  Plastic Pollution Coalition

Preface:
My Ocean,
My Planet

We'd woken before dawn to catch the ultra-low tides and hike along the rocky tip of a slender peninsula pointing like an arrow into the wild waves of the Pacific Ocean. A pristine passage, normally denied by pounding California breakers, had briefly opened to reveal inter-tidal wonders usually submerged. This ephemeral sliver of beach is only accessible a few times a year when the tides dip into the negative.

We had dropped one car at the southern end of the hike as dawn's first light peeked over the coastal mountains, parking at the northernmost access point. Soon our small band, my husband, children and friends, and I, would be exploring tidepools normally shrouded with foamy surf and climbing through rocky keyholes aquatically worn into the caves. This cold hike called for wetsuit bottoms, fleece underlayers, spray jackets, and thick-soled water shoes. We put on our gear and then fueled up with hard-boiled eggs, fruit, and hot coffee.

Our plan was to travel a stretch of California rarely seen, to discover the beauty of this pro-tected stretch of unsullied coastline. Our hearts soared when we found black metamorphic rocks lining our path. They were studded with brilliant orange sea stars bigger than our hands. Muscu-lar bull kelp and a tapestry of iridescent seaweed shimmered at our feet. Nubby black mussels blan-keted the rocks like chain mail armor, warding us away from the higher, drier routes, and into the slippery tide pools that were churning like wash-ing machines with rhythmic swells. There, we were greeted by underwater fields of blossoming sea anemones with their turquoise mouths and tentacles ringed by army-green polyps hungrily gaping to the sky in hopes of snaring a passer-by.

This bountiful marine beauty was matched by a symphony of roaring waves, barking sea lions, and cawing seagulls. Immersed in an oceanic soundscape, our eyes, ears, and hearts felt cradled in nature's sovereignty. Our suburban lives seemed light-years away.

But then, our attention shifted…and our hearts sank.

We caught sight of a rainbow made of thousands, probably hundreds of thousands, of brightly colored plastic objects in all sizes and shapes that had washed ashore and mounded along the foot of the 200-foot tall cliffs. There was no escaping the reality that our idyllic adventure had hit a dead-end. Instead of nature's beauty, we were flanked by mountains of plastic.

The constant rhythm of the Pacific waves marked the closing of our tidal window and of our marine adventure. Like a metronome counting down, it reminded us with each incoming swell that the time allotted us on this sliver of land was fast closing. We had to move forward to escape getting trapped. In just a moment or two the powerful ocean would swallow the strip of beach we were borrowing for our marine exploration.

Staying past our welcome was decidedly unwise, but we had to do something about all the plastic that had been choked up by the ocean.

There was no time for regrets, for recriminations, for jovial fake promises that we'd surely come back another day when we were better equipped, had more money or people or equipment or time. We filled our arms and buckets with what the sea had spit out, like gardeners pulling psychedelic, run-amok weeds from a long-forgotten, untended rock garden. Hauling flip flops, fishing floats, trawling lines, toothbrushes, tampon applicators, buckets, baskets, water jugs, and endless broken bits of plastic from every room and part of human life that lay littering our path, we beat our way down the beach to safe passage.

We trudged through sand dunes dusted with minute confetti-like plastic specks too small to gather, like the leftovers of a massive beach party gone wild. Arms and hearts heavy, hardly having made a dent, we wondered if our efforts had been futile, if we'd made a measurable difference.

Our clean-up efforts were admittedly a drop in the proverbial bucket, yet we were joyful for having acted on our love for the ocean and I knew we would gladly return to do it all over again. Love is a force as powerful and unstoppable as the tides and breakers of the ocean.

We do what we can to protect what we love.

—SANDRA ANN HARRIS,
Mother, Seeker, Environmentalist,
and Entrepreneur

Introduction

Hello! It's great to meet you. I'm Sandra. Thank you so much for the opportunity to share with you my plastic-free journey. I'm a mother of two, a wife, an environmentalist, sailor, spiritualist, daughter, activist, and accidental zero-waste entrepreneur based in the San Francisco Bay Area of California.

Seventeen years ago, getting rid of plastic became my passion project, my purpose, and my livelihood. Along the way, I have learned a tremendous amount about plastic pollution, including the health and environmental hazards of this petroleum-based material. I have also discovered many affordable and easy-to-implement hacks to help everyday people say goodbye to plastic.

So much has changed when it comes to living a plastic-free life, even just over the last five years. Earlier books on this subject required extensive product recipes and handicraft tutorials to "Mac-Gyver" homemade, labor-intensive, plastic-free products and solutions. The marketplace has luckily evolved and plastic-free solutions, though perhaps not terribly easy to find on your own, are now widely available online and in stores. Furthermore, commonsense solutions our grandparents relied on, like paper straws and glass and steel food storage are flowing back into vogue. The wisdom of our elders and indigenous peoples who've come before us has been made relevant again by the urgency of our crisis.

I'm not going to ask you to do anything I wouldn't do myself, like concocting personal care products, whipping up your own butter, fabricating your own wax wraps or mixing DIY household cleaners. As a busy mom with full-time employment, it has been critical that saying goodbye to plastic adds joy, ease, beauty and value to my life—not guilt or stress.

What I will be sharing with you, is how I successfully transitioned my family into a lifestyle that is very lean on plastics. I will tell how I mustered the courage to found my own business,

ECOlunchbox, at my kitchen table in 2008 in order to help other families reduce their dependence on plastics. I will take you room by room and show you all the tips, hacks, and swaps I have learned that will up your plastic-free game. Just by reading this book, you will learn how to easily say good-bye to up to three-quarters of the plastics you are using, starting with the lowest-hanging fruit on the plastic tree: single-use plastic packaging.

Whether you have just woken up to the devastating realities of plastic pollution and want to get up to speed quickly, or you've been on the zero-waste journey for a while and want to level up, this book is for you. Maybe some plastic-free zealot in your life has gifted you this book and you don't want to upset them by not reading it. No matter the reason, I sincerely believe you will find something of value in these pages that will help shift your habits and begin making changes step by step, room by room, towards being part of the plastic pollution solution.

My Plastic Lightbulb Moment

Let me take you all the way back to the beginning of my journey with plastic, or what I call my "plastic lightbulb" moment.

It was 2003 and I hadn't given plastic much thought, except for those horrifying plastic six-pack beverage rings, the 1970's premier flash-point for ocean conservation. Yet despite 50 years having passed, the problem of animals getting entangled in these deadly plastic six-pack rings persisted. So I'd kept on snipping these rings with scissors before discarding to protect marine life downstream. I also had a few other good plastic habits, like washing and re-using plastic sandwich baggies and always recycling. At the time, these steps seemed good enough.

As I look back after 17 years of joyfully and per-sistently saying goodbye to the plastic in my life, I can still sympathize with the young mom I was at the time. She didn't know what I know now about plastic. Her responsibilities were many and plastic wasn't high on her priority list. In fact, it wasn't on her radar at all.

Something changed the day my three-year-old son Niko brought home his half-eaten lunch from preschool. Normally, he brought home an empty lunch box, but that day, it looked like a bomb had gone off in his padded, insulated tote. Inside was a jumble of half-eaten foods mixed with torn plastics. His smushed sandwich with a couple of bites gone was mangled in a plastic Ziploc. Half of his cheese stick was still stuck in its plastic sleeve. Gross! And what was all that sticky wet stuff? Ah, it was the apple juice trickling out of the mini plastic straw in the drink box. I vividly recall peering down into that vinyl insulated tote wondering what the heck had happened to the tidy lunchtime goodness I'd packed with love that morning. Even the goldfish crackers were dissolving into mush, victims of the leaky juice box.

I was irritated at the school for sending Niko's leftovers and trash back home with him. Couldn't they have at least thrown this mess away rather than stuffing it back in his lunchbox and making it my problem? Wasn't I paying the preschool to make my life easier and to free me up to work? And now I had to take care of this plastic garbage disaster!

Ticked off that I had one more thing to deal with, I resentfully dumped the entire plasticky lot into my garbage can and scrubbed the padded lunch tote out for the next day. I thought to myself: *Couldn't someone else do all this? Maybe it was just a fluke and they'd take care of his lunch waste at the school the next day.* Fortunately (no, this isn't a typo), the trash from Niko's lunch just kept coming home with him, and finally—sometimes we need to get the message more than once before we hear it—I realized that this plastic mess really was my problem to solve after all. I couldn't get out of it.

That was the moment that I woke up to the perils of plastic. (I'm curious, dear reader, about what woke you up?) As you read my story, I invite you to reflect on your own personal "plastic lightbulb" moment that has either already happened or is likely to show up now that you're training your focus on reducing plastics in your life.

Throwing Money Away?

Being the curious sort, and a former investigative journalist, I started to ask around about the school's trash policy and soon found out that the preschool director was on the cheap side. (The fees didn't feel cheap, however). Apparently, her garbage bill was cutting into her profits and, while she wasn't particularly environmentally minded, she didn't like to waste money on garbage. And so she had implemented a zero-waste program: families who packed in waste also had to pack it out and throw it away in their own garbage cans.

Even though I didn't like having to deal with the waste, I realized the preschool director had a valid fiscal point of view. Paying for expensive garbage service was putting money in the trash. Taking it a step further, I penciled out the cost of the pre-packaged lunch foods, like yogurt squeezes, applesauce packs, and juice boxes with disposable straws, comparing the per-ounce costs of these foods in packaging against buying them in bulk. (I'm wondering, dear reader, if you might also like to save a little green by going green?)

The math had convinced me that even though it would be more work for me in terms of packing and cleaning, I needed to stop using so many pre-packaged foods and make a switch to reusable containers. So I endeavored to put together a reusable lunch set for my son Niko. However, this was 2003, and there weren't many options out there for families yet.

Goodbye Juice Box

The first thing I did was immediately ditch the juice boxes. Made from a mix of paperboard and plastic, the boxes and little straws weren't recyclable so they had to be trashed. They weren't resealable either, so the leaking was making a big mess for me. Our family had large one-liter plastic water bottles that we used when we were backpacking, kayaking and doing other outdoorsy activities, but we kept them in the attic and only took them out for special occasions. Around town we hadn't yet gotten into the habit of using small reusable bottles to avert dependence on pre-packaged drinks.

Since we are an outdoor-loving family, it was natural for me to head over to REI, the outdoor retailer, to scout out some options and pick up a couple of smaller hard plastic water bottles.

There were no drink containers available without plastic. Natural grocery and children supply stores didn't even stock reusable bottles at that time. Other than baby bottles for infants and no-spill sippy cups, personal reusable water bottles had not caught on yet. Thankfully, 17 years later, it's a no-brainer to bring one's own water bottle wherever you go. This wonderful habit has caught on strongly in recent years, most widely in coastal communities and university towns where environmental and health awareness is heightened. Yes, in Virginia (and in a whole bunch of other states), single-use plastic water bottles are being phased out! We are collectively learning and responding to the plastic pollution crisis already! But with more than 35 billion single-use plastic bottles still thrown away every year in the United States, there is definitely more work to be done.

I was thrilled the following year in 2004 to find stainless steel water bottles on the shelves at

REI! Made by Klean Kanteen, these metal water bottles were first to market. Stainless steel is a great non-toxic, non-leaching, non-corrosive, and strong material, so I picked up a couple of the kid-size water bottles for my son. They worked out so well for us, I bought one for myself, but I kept using the plastic ones, too, since they were supposedly non-toxic made from a safe, rigid plastic.

Plastic-Free Lunch Box Quest

After ditching pre-packaged foods, I began portioning lunch entrées and side dishes from bulk purchases. I stocked up on family-size packaged dry goods and large plastic tubs and glass jars of wet foods, like yogurt and applesauce, to reduce packaging waste. However, a couple of years had passed since 2003 when I had started my plastic-free journey and I still hadn't found a non-toxic container that wouldn't leach chemicals into my children's lunches.

One of my biggest unanswered questions was: What could I pack my kids' lunch in that wasn't made out of plastic?

I went out into the marketplace to find plastic-free food containers made out of stainless steel that we could pair with the metal water bottles we'd grown to love and trust. I couldn't think of a better, safer material for our family's food containers but I was I sadly disappointed when I came back empty-handed. I simply couldn't find anything available without plastic. I settled on a few, very small Tupperware containers made out of rigid plastic because I thought this type of plastic was less likely to have toxins than soft plastics like Ziplocs. At least they were zero waste and leak-proof so I wouldn't have to deal with a huge, soggy mess of jumbled food when he got home.

Complicating matters, we soon learned Niko was not very good about opening those little plastic containers with tight, no-leak lids. On top of that, my son was a late talker and he would not ask his teachers for help with the Tupperware. Instead, he simply stopped eating at school. He would come home with all of his containers still packed with food because he hadn't been able to open his containers. I spoke with his teachers and requested that they keep an extra eye on him at lunch time and help him open his containers. Meanwhile, I went in search of a better container solution.

I was aware that in India there was a practice of packing lunches in multi-level steel containers with clips called tiffins. (If you, dear reader, like foreign films and romance, there's a great one focused on the tiffin traditions of India called *The Lunchbox*.) I packed Niko and his younger sister Mabel into our station wagon and drove to the Fremont area where there was a high population of Indian immigrants. I was on the hunt for an Indian grocery store that carried these so-called tiffins.

I scored richly when it came to rices, spices and salty snacks, but hours into my search, my wee ones were ready for naps and I still hadn't struck gold in my hunt for a tiffin. Finally, a sari-clad shopkeeper waved me to the back of her store to check an overlooked bottom shelf. That's where I found a few sad, dented, and dusty stainless-steel food containers. They were about five inches round with two stacked layers and flimsy clips. I decided to give them a try.

Back at home, my husband and I used pliers to adjust the clips (not too loose to fall off and not too tight to keep Niko from accessing his food) used a miter sander to smooth sharp weld, and gave them a hot soapy scrub. Voila! We ecstatically filled the tiffins up with snacks and showed Niko how to open and close his new lunch boxes. Soon his little hands had skillfully mastered the clips.

But alas, the size, configuration, and quality of these tiffins were not quite right for our needs.

Many Indian tiffins are round and stackable so that rice, dal and vegetable curries can all be packed separately, and at lunchtime the tins can be laid out together as a mix and match meal. But a small rectangular container would have been ideal for Niko's half-a-sandwich lunch and side dishes.

A Business is Born

It wasn't until several years later in 2008 when I returned to REI to buy more metal water bottles that I saw a sight that motivated me to finally start my plastic-free business ECOlunchbox. Weirdly, an entire shelf next to the metal water bottles was completely empty. A sign said "Recall" and noted that the plastic bottles that used to be on that shelf contained a chemical called BPA that REI believed to be unsafe for consumers. My curiosity was piqued. A recall on our favorite brand of reusable plastic water bottles? Why? (I'm wondering, dear reader, if you are concerned about safeguarding your health as I am? This can be a motivator for plastic-free lifestyle change as well.)

It turned out that the plastic water bottle brand we'd been purchasing for decades had tested positive for bisphenol-A (BPA). Little known to most consumers, BPA was developed in 1891 as an artificial estrogen. It was tested as a possible hormonal birth control for women but deemed ineffective, so its makers sold it to the plastics industry as an additive to enhance the rigidity of plastics like polycarbonate.

I was spurred by the startling recall to dive even more deeply into my own research around bisphenol-A. I had thought that squeezy plastics were the most "leachy" so I'd continued to use rigid plastics. Now, I needed to know whether this chemical found in rigid plastics posed health risks to my son and daughter, who were now 8 and 5. I was shocked to learn that the recalled plastic water bottles had leached unhealthy levels of this estrogen-mimicking chemical into liquids. I wondered, *'How had this been allowed to happen?'* In my research I had learned that exposure to estrogen-mimicking chemicals, like BPA, is a health risk to both boys and girls.

Until the recall, I had naively assumed that government regulator would not allow unsafe chemicals in consumer products. Wasn't the U.S. Food and Drug Administration charged with protecting the public from health risks? (I'm curious, dear reader, if you also had the same impression that our health agencies would ban products with unhealthy toxins?) It would take many more years before U.S. agencies caught up with the Canadian and European health officials that had already started to restrict and ban BPA, especially in children's products.

A deep distrust for consumer products made from plastic welled up inside of me. I had small children and a planet under my care; the stakes were high. I felt like I was on a health and environmental journey with no roadmap, bobbing in the waves, blown by confusing winds and struggling to find safe passage for my family and planet. And so I set out to chart my own plastic-free path.

Motivated by this unexpected recall and inspired by our Indian tiffins, I resolved to start a mission-based, plastic-free company to help families like ours reduce their dependence on plastics at lunchtime. If our family needed to pack plastic-free lunches, I guessed others would, too. It was a low-tech response to a modern problem inspired by the time-honored tiffin tradition in South Asia as well as in numerous other eastern and western countries dating back for generations. In Arab countries, reusable lunch tins are called safartas ("travel bowls" in Turkish); in the Philippines, báon ("packed lunch"); in Hungry éthordó ("food carrier"). In Japan they use bento boxes while workers in the United States have long used metal lunch pails.

When I launched in 2008, my business plan was to take the tried-and-true tradition of metal lunch boxes and make it new again for modern consumers. So we created new products to fit larger one-pot meals like grain bowls, pasta dishes, and salads. We developed rectangular-shaped lunch boxes with nesting containers that fit easily into backpacks and other rectangular totes, adding silicone gaskets and soft-close clips so they wouldn't leak when toted to school or work. We popped color and inspirational ocean motifs onto the leak-proof lids of our Blue Water Bento collection, visually connecting our user community to their deep love for Big Blue.

I'm thrilled that over the last decade we've helped hundreds of thousands of people say goodbye to plastic at lunchtime. People are finally getting the message loud and clear that plastic pollution has got to stop. Better late than never.

How To Use This Book

For the past 17 years, I've been obsessively ferreting out lifestyle solutions to reduce my family's dependence on plastics. I've been single-mindedly eating, praying, and loving all things related to plastic-free living for many years. Choosing to use stainless steel water bottles and launching my company ECOlunchbox in 2008 to make plastic-free, steel food container solutions available for my own family and the world is just the tip of the iceberg. I'm thrilled to share myriad approaches to saying goodbye to unnecessary plastic.

When it comes to giving plastic the boot, there's no reason to feel overwhelmed. You too can be part of the solution to plastic pollution. I invite you to dive in by introducing you room by room to many easy, cost-effective strategies you can press into action in your everyday life. I have done the legwork to find easy lifestyle swaps so you don't have to. Living with less plastic is not only cheaper, it's beautiful and delightfully pleasurable.

Whether you are just starting to remove plastic from your life or are already on the path and ready to crack a few of the tougher plastic challenges in your life, this book is for you.

I have dedicated most of the chapters in this book to the rooms in your home: kitchen, bathroom, bedroom, dining room, entertainment rooms, and office. For each, I identify the main plastic offenders with a focus on the biggest culprits—single-use plastic and packaging that isn't recyclable. I offer tips for removing these items from your home, swapping them with eco-friendly and non-toxic alternatives, and I also provide simple practices that you can incorporate to minimize the amount of plastic waste that you generate.

I wrote these tips for readers at various stages of their journey. There are some basics in this book for beginners, but if you've been around the plastic-free block a time or two already, I have included some lesser-known, more "advanced" plastic-free living strategies. Some readers may be surprised, for example, to learn that they are literally wearing plastic every day. Did you know that most synthetic textiles are made from plastics? Textile waste is a huge, hidden problem when it comes to plastic pollution. And one of the toughest pain points when it comes to saying goodbye to plastics resides in your wardrobe and your related laundry habits. Why on earth are the solutions that we rely on to keep our clothing and homes clean actually dirtying our waters with micro plastics and packaged wastefully in plastic? Something can and must be done about this problem in your closet—allow me to be your guide through the Closet & Clothing and Laundry Room & Cleaning chapters.

Last, I touch on an area that is not a room but a beloved activity that for many of us feels really out of our control when it comes to plastic waste: travel. So much packaging for so many tiny travel-sized items! And what about eating on the go without creating a mountain of single-use plastic waste? Have no fear; I'll show you how to create a waste-free travel kit that will not only be good for the planet, but will also make packing for your next trip a smoother process and more cost-effective.

I suggest starting in whatever area of your life feels right to you. As environmental activist, Jane Goodall put it, "What you do makes a difference, and you have to decide what kind of a difference you want to make." I started my journey making a plastic-free difference in my kitchen with food storage but you get to pick your own plastic-free path. Where will you have the most fun making a difference swapping out plastics?

And remember, Rome wasn't built in a day. The same is true for your plastic-free home. It's going to take some time to transition but with patience and persistence you can easily weed plastic out of your home and create a new lifestyle that's dramatically leaner when it comes to plastic usage. The key to success is adopting a playful, incremental approach. No blaming! No shaming! Just start, like you would at a beach clean-up, rooting out each needless piece of plastic one by one, room by room. I think you'll be surprised when you learn how we as a society have become so senselessly overdependent on plastic in the last 50 years when there are so many great alternatives available to us.

Ready to dive in? Skip ahead a couple chapters to learn about my favorite plastic-free tools. I'll show you how to create your very own toolkit with all the everyday gear you will need to begin or continue your mission to live a plastic-free life, and head to your favorite room to start rooting out the unnecessary plastic in your home. At the end of the book, you'll also find a slew of resources to help you level up on your plastic-free game.

Maybe you're still not convinced of the magnitude of plastic pollution and want to learn more about the issue to get your plastic-free engines revved for takeoff? If that's the case, proceed directly to the next chapter. Do not pass go, fill up your reusable tea mug, and give me a few precious minutes to educate you about the origins of the plastic pollution crisis. Hopefully, I can convince you to join us in adopting a plastic-free lifestyle.

With this book, I invite you to join me and the hundreds of thousands of people worldwide who have made the decision to minimize their use of unnecessary plastic and reduce plastic waste. I will educate you about the many factors contributing to the devastating problem of plastic pollution, and show you all the tips and hacks I have learned to make getting rid of plastic fun and easy. Most importantly, I'll urge you to shake off any fear, apathy, or blame that might be holding you back from activating around this global crisis, and be your guide in saying goodbye to the massive amounts of needless plastic that has invaded our daily lives.

Trust me, living with less plastic is not only cheaper, it is beautiful and delightfully pleasurable.

An SOS To The World

The ocean has been romanticized as the infinite provider of dreams and resources—and the receiver of all our garbage for as long as I can remember. Take for instance the 1979 hit song *Message In A Bottle* that was an uncanny (and unintentional) foreshadowing of the global crisis we are confronting today. I remember listening to the popular song by the British rock band The Police sing the lyrics about a person discovering "a hundred billion" bottles washed up on an island.

As I belted out the catchy refrain "I'll send an SOS to the world" again and again, I never dreamed we'd actually have billions of plastic water bottles polluting our oceans. In those moments, the song was all about me and my angst. Looking back, I realize I never really heard the song's message from the ocean's perspective. Our beloved ocean and her SOS was far from mind.

With plastic water bottles and straws now the poster children of the plastic pollution movement, this poignant song has a whole new meaning for me. Finally, we are hearing the SOS message our ocean has been sending for more than four decades.

It wasn't on anyone's mind in 1979 that billions of plastic bottles were actually building up in our seas. In fact, I was so clueless back then that I even added to the plastic waste in our oceans. On purpose! Several times! As part of an ongoing school project, I threw bottles containing messages into the ocean with the hope that someone in a faraway land might recover them and send back a postcard saying hello from someplace exciting. I also sent up helium balloons with messages, though nowhere near the 99 popularized by German rock star Nena in the 1984 pop hit *99 Red Balloons* or the thousands set free at rock concerts "'til one by one, they were gone," as the song goes.

There has long been a mindless throw-away culture that romanticizes casting objects into mysterious neverlands to be received by intriguing strangers. But who actually received our bottles, balloons, and messages? Our oceans. And when they were spit back out onto our beaches, we didn't listen.

We can't ignore our ocean's SOS calls any longer. The tsunami of plastic flooding our oceans is choking our marine ecosystems with dire consequences for humanity and marine life. Scientists have discovered 11 swirling accumulations of plastic debris, including a huge ocean gyre in the Pacific Ocean between Hawaii and Alaska, which they've dubbed the "Great Pacific Garbage Patch."[1] I remember feeling deeply saddened when I first saw pictures of the water samples taken by Captain Charles Moore, founder of Algalita, a marine debris research and educational non-profit. Lurking beneath the tropical ocean's gorgeous surface, Moore had discovered by use of trawling nets a horrifying underwater smog made up of trillions of pieces of brightly colored plastic particles. The news was akin to hearing, for example, that scientists had verified UFOs, Big Foot, or the Loch Ness Monster. Naturally, at first many people were skeptical and chalked the news up to exaggeration.

To educate others about the garbage patch at school science fairs and Earth Day events, my children and I would bring a galvanized stainless steel tub, fill it with water, and add cut up pieces of recyclable plastic waste from our home. To try and emulate the Great Pacific Garbage Patch, we'd vigorously stir the plastic-filled soup with a big spoon to emulate the powerful marine gyres where winds and waves collect the non-biodegradable plastic waste in the the Pacific Ocean between the Hawaiian Islands and Alaska. (Watch the swirling water next time you drain your tub after a bath to envision these spiraling currents.) Then we would invite children to pick their favorite animal from a basket of plastic bath toys we had on hand and plop it into the soup, imagining how it might be for marine animals to live in an ocean with more plastic than fish—as scientists have predicted will happen by the year 2050.[2]

Then, we'd offer a little fishing net to our students so they could scoop into our mini gyre and attempt to rescue their critter. (What's your favorite marine animal, dear reader, that you'd like to save?). To further bring home the point, we'd pass around brittle pieces of washed ashore ocean plastics, like toothbrushes, pieces of flip flops, partial broken water bottles, caps, combs, and cigarette lighters so people could touch, feel, and understand the magnitude of plastic waste accumulation in our seas. In little vials from a research non-profit called the 5 Gyres Institute, we showed brightly colored micro bits of marine plastics that we now know are insidiously making their way up the food chain. Then we talked to them about how to help solve this problem by reducing their use and disposal of unnecessary plastics.

In an expedition journal entry written by Captain Moore, explorer of the plastic gyres, he colorfully recounts his impressions of these microplastics in nature and his subsequent overwhelming realization of the massive scope of the pollution.[3]

"Remember eating sprinkles on cupcakes as a kid?" Moore recounts. "The tiny little colorful sugary beads…so colorful and delicious and always associated with good times…! But, if you spilled them, man oh man, what a task it was to clean up all those hundreds of colorful tiny sprinkles."

Getting the plastic bottles, balloons and everything else into the ocean was easy, but, as Captain Moore points out, it is really difficult to get them back out. Studies tell us that each year more than eight million tons of plastic leaks into the ocean—the equivalent of dumping the contents of one garbage truck into the ocean every minute. If no action is taken, this number is expected to double to two per minute by 2030 and four per minute by 2050.[4]

Yes, But I Recycle!

Recycling has been heralded for decades as the panacea for plastic dependence, with feel-good products made from recycled plastic like polyester fleece jackets, skateboards, sunglasses, shoes, and toys. Indeed, it's admirable these products are being made and old water bottles and fishing nets are finding a value in the marketplace that averts them from disposal in our landfills or in our oceans. The trouble is that lots of dirty, low-quality, or non-conforming plastic, such as items without sorting codes stamped on the bottom, have never been able to be recycled. Their low value combined with the high cost of converting them into a recycled end product means consumers have been pulling the plastic wool over their eyes for decades.

In fact, only 1–5 percent of global discarded plastics have ever really been recycled and, despite growing demand for the service, recycling rates are declining. For three decades China and Hong Kong had imported about three-quarters of the world's traded plastic waste. Consumers felt no remorse in using plastic, because, after all, it was being recycled into new products, right? That changed when China jammed the works of recycling programs around the world by shutting down what had been the industry's biggest market.

Enacted in January 2018, China's "National Sword" environmental policy banned the import of most plastics and other materials headed for the nation's recycling processors. The world is unequipped to handle the onslaught of waste that would normally have been shipped to China for recycling. Private and municipal recycling programs that depended on sale of discarded plastics to China have resorted to burying and burning the waste, with serious carbon emissions consequences. Others have gone out of business.

Even now in the face of the Chinese ban and the shrinking market for recycled plastics, many consumers keep falsely citing recycling as an excuse for their overreliance on plastics, especially packaging and single-use plastics that comprise more than half of the plastics waste stream. Little do they know that their discarded plastics are likely ending up buried, burned, or shipped overseas to unknown fates.

Plastic, Plastic Everywhere

I was recently visiting our ECOlunchbox manufacturing facilities in Chennai, India, to meet with our business partners who make our lunch boxes when I found myself unexpectedly surrounded by plastic waste. I caught something pink flying by out of the corner of my eye. Just a few moments later, something yellow pulled my attention as it drifted away. I soon realized these weren't tropical birds; they were plastic bags.

I ventured outside on the second story to assess my surroundings. All around our steel factory, which was dedicated to helping reduce families' dependence on plastics, I could see piles of discarded plastic. We were surrounded by uncontrolled plastic waste accumulated by sorting companies who were presumably going to divert some of the plastic to recycling facilities. There was no one working the plastic that day. The only force in action was the wind.

Heading to lunch, we beat our way downtown through thick, cacophonous traffic, passing piles of plastic bags, bottles, wrappers, and other single-use plastics. Scrawny cows and dogs picked through the plastic rubbish looking for scraps of food. Uncontrolled plastic waste was everywhere and trash cans were non-existent. We arrived at a pleasant hole-in-the-wall restaurant specializing in *idlis*, South Indian steamed rice cakes. These dollar-sized cakes were traditionally served on vibrant jade-colored biodegradable palm leaves.

White and fluffy, the *idlis* cakes were the perfect foil for coconut chutney and *samber* Indian vegetable stew. Again and again we dipped our *idlis* into sauces served in little cups made out of dried leaves and pressed into mini ramekins. We ate with the ultimate reusable utensils: our fingers. In lieu of napkins, there was a sink with soapy water for hand washing.

Our longtime ECOlunchbox business partners in India are vegans and delight in sharing with me their delicious cuisine when I visit. Their partnership and faith in our plastic-free mission since the company's early days has made my work as a plastic-free entrepreneur and activist possible. As we shared this delicious, zero-waste vegan feast, my partners gently encouraged me to give up meat, dairy, eggs and even honey (I'm a beekeeper!) for animal rights considerations. Without directly criticizing my meat eating, they quietly convinced me that meat wasn't needed to have a fabulous flavorful meal.

As the workday drew to a close and dusk gathered in, we swung by their home to gather up their young sons for a beach outing. We joined thousands of other Indian families along the Bay of Bengal beach to play in the water and enjoy street food snacks. Weaving in and out of crowds of multigenerational families were hundreds of entrepreneurial vendors hawking rainbow-colored saber light sticks, hot pink cotton candy, mylar balloons, ice creams in plastic wrappers, and many fried and salted street snacks in plastic baggies.

We sat down to chat and play with the children, as we all nibbled away, emptying the plastic sacks of our treats. I could see numerous plastic baggies catch the wind all around us and float away with the waves. I snatched a couple and stuck them in my pocket, but thousands more were out of reach.

The plastic waste was so needless. These very same snacks had been packaged for generations in banana leaves, old newspaper, and other biodegradable, plant-based materials. Tossing aside these biodegradable wrappers brought little consequence, as they were easily composted, leaving little trace. However, when cheap omnipresent plastic became widely available, it was taken up by vendors with enthusiasm. The plastic baggies looked so clean and modern, causing less spoilage and contamination since the food stayed cleaner and fresher in plastic. The reasons for the changeover to plastic seemed positive at the time, but unfortunately consumers didn't change their habits accordingly.

Instead of just throwing banana leaf wrappers to the ground to harmlessly biodegrade, consumers in India and many other places with traditionally sustainable approaches to single-use packaging have continued throwing away their snack packaging even though it is now made of non-biodegradable plastic. Worse, even if these beach-goers had wanted to throw their baggies in the trash, it would be nearly impossible to find a public trash can. In places like this beach we were visiting, the only trash cans to be found were a 10-minute walk away in the parking areas—and they were overflowing.

Not My Fault, Not My Problem?

Despite the glaring issues with uncontrolled plastic waste in the developing world, it's a mistake to pin all the blame for the plastic pollution crisis on just a portion of the global population. This pollution belongs to all of us everywhere whether rich or poor, brown or white.

First-world waste producers brag that only one percent of plastic marine debris washes into the oceans from their shores.[5] Yet citizens of these same countries are some of the heaviest personal plastic users and have no qualms about shipping their plastic garbage overseas for someone else to deal with. Out of sight, out of mind.

Yes, ten times as much of the plastic in our oceans originates from river inputs in Asia than from more developed nations, but ten times as much plastic is used and disposed of in those developed nations than in Asia. In Europe and the United States, citizens are disposing a pound of plastic daily as compared to less than a tenth of that amount in numerous developing countries.

Finger pointing is an instinctive human response to suffering, but now isn't the time for recriminations. We all live here together in this borderless global ecosystem called Earth.

Vietnamese Buddhist monk, Thich Nhat Hanh, inspires us to seek solutions collectively with his mantra of connectedness:

"You carry Mother Earth within you. She is not outside of you. Mother Earth is not just your environment. In that insight of inter-being, it is possible to have real communication with the Earth, which is the highest form of prayer. In that kind of relationship you have enough love, strength and awakening in order to change your life. Fear, separation, hate and anger come from the wrong view that you and the Earth are two separate entities, that the Earth is only the environment. That is a dualistic way of seeing."

In our shared ecosystem, we're all being flooded with perilous plastic pollution from overuse of the material and mismanagement of its waste. We're all at fault and it's all of our problem. Solving this issue will take work from everyone. In caring for Mother Earth, we care for ourselves and for each other. I wonder, dear readers, are you ready to be a part of the solution to save her from the plastic crisis? Read on to find out how you can do your part to reduce the amount of plastic finding its way from your hands into our beloved oceans. We will start by putting together your plastic-free toolkit.

My Favorite Plastic-Free Tools

Before we begin our room by room journey to rid your home of plastic, let's take a moment to tool you up for a plastic-free life on the go. When you're living plastic-free in a world filled with plastic conveniences, you have to have a few go-to reusable items up your sleeve—or in your purse, pocket, or wherever. For those of us who are saying goodbye to plastic, here are the tools you'll need to aid you on your quest.

The funny thing about saying goodbye to plastic is that it's not hard-- as long as you plan ahead. A little forethought goes a long way towards having the power to refuse plastic waste associated with purchasing to-go food items. Start by setting your sights on stopping the use of single-use plastic utensils, straws, coffee cups, cold beverage containers and other omnipresent take-out containers.

To avoid unexpected wasteful surprises on the go, I've learned to have various zero-waste supplies squirrelled away in a few different locations such as in my purse (tiny items like a spork and a foldable straw), my travel backpack (add drink and food containers), and my car trunk (a box stocked with a bunch of clean reusables). If you use public transit, stock a bigger stash at your office, in a school locker, or another location that makes sense for you. This way, when one source runs out, you can usually find a back-up. The key is to wash and replace the items after use so you're always stocked and ready.

Here are the essentials I rely on in my plastic-free toolkit:

- **Hot Beverage Container:** Wide-mouth insulated metal beverage container or a regular ceramic mug for hot to-go beverages like coffee and tea. Baristas need the wide-mouth for easy filling.
- **Cold Beverage Container:** Single-walled, lightweight metal or glass water bottle for bring-your-own (BYO) water and to-go cold beverages. If you're travelling and need to pack light,

just bring the insulated tumbler and it can serve a dual purpose, but often it's nice to have water and be able to order a coffee or another to-go drink without emptying your reusable bottle.

- **Straw & Brush:** Reusable straw made from glass, steel, bamboo, silicone, or other non-plastic option. For reusable straws, don't forget to also get a straw brush for on-the-go cleaning. I love glass straws because you can always see if they're clean and they really aren't as breakable as you might think, especially if carried in a sleeve. You might also like some single-use biodegradable straws in your toolkit made from paper or wheat hay so you can skip the hassle of cleaning it after use.

- **Mason Jar:** A wide-mouth mason jar (32 oz. or bigger) with a screw-on lid, for easy transport of smoothies and other to-go treats like acai bowls, salads, grain bowls, and more.

- **Utensils:** Reusable utensils for fast casual dining out: fork, spoon, chopsticks, butter knife, and a small knife (either sharp for cutting or dull for spreading or one of each) safely wrapped in a cotton napkin or toted in a utensil carrier. Check for mismatched utensils at the back of your kitchen drawer or reach out to friends and neighbors for their extras. You can also find nice travel sets for sale which include Western utensils and chopsticks, all made out of bamboo and sold in cotton roll-up totes.

- **Nesting Containers:** A few reusable containers, including at least one that's 48 oz. or bigger. These will come in super handy for restaurant leftovers, take-out orders, and zero-waste bulk shopping (more on that in the Kitchen chapter.) For compact carrying, try to get a set with several containers in a variety of sizes that nest inside each other like Russian dolls.

- **Tiny Bag:** Very small reusable shopping bag that stuffs into its own micro sack. Ideally, it's small enough to be on your keychain, so you can have it with you wherever you go.

- **Bags or Boxes:** Several grocery box totes or bags. Flat-bottom, foldable grocery boxes are great for picking up to-go food because your food containers will sit flat, retaining the plating and lessening the risk of any spillage. (More on the upside of using foldable boxes for bulk shopping trips in the Kitchen chapter.)

You probably already have many of these items in your home. If not, thrift stores and garage sales are great affordable options for purchasing many of them. A natural grocery store is another great source of eco-friendly reusable items.

As a side note, you may have heard about the zero-waste "superheroes" who've reduced their annual waste to as little as one pint-size jar. Sometimes they're pictured in elegant Instagram photos displaying a little pile of trash that fits in the palm of their hand. If you're like me, you might feel like you can never live up to this high standard. Shake off these self-depreciating emotions; they aren't useful. Be inspired by their determination. These zealots are the Michael Jordans of the plastic-free lifestyle. They're showing us that it's possible to set sights high and score big for the environment.

Sometimes you are going to fall short of whatever sights you have set for yourself, I know I have. We've all had instances at the front of the grocery store line when we realize we left our reusable bags in the car…again. I've broken a sweat racing to and from my car, trying to get back to the check-out counter without holding up the line. It happens. You'd be surprised at how understanding check-out clerks and shoppers can be if you ask them to start ringing up your order while you dash out to the car to get those forgotten bags. They often relate saying "That happens to me too."

If a situation occurs in which running to fetch your bags is not an option, please don't sweat it. Skip the personal trip down guilt lane and either buy yourself a couple of new reusable shopping bags or opt for a paper bag.

Remind yourself that you are learning and your intention is to say goodbye to more and more plastic as time goes by and as you become more expert in plastic-free living. By loving ourselves as much as we love our planet, we find within ourselves the energy needed to persist in removing needless plastic from our lives.

And now, with toolkit in hand, let's move on to my passion project: the kitchen.

Kitchen & Shopping

We all have areas of special interests that make our hearts sing. For me it was my kids' homemade lunches. I loved the challenge of eradicating plastic from lunch time. For others, shopping at the farmers' market and buying things in bulk at the grocery store are fun ways for them to put their values into practice.

My plastic-free journey began in the kitchen because I didn't think it was safe to have my foods touching so much plastic. I didn't like the idea of my kids' lunch containers and water bottles leaching harmful chemicals like the pseudo-estrogen bisphenol-A (BPA) into what they ate and drank.

The first thing I did was buy a stainless steel water bottle and stop using Ziploc baggies and the other soft, squeezy plastics believed to be the most toxic. Using this as my foundation, I started my company ECOlunchbox to make plastic-free food containers. Once I tackled my Tupperware drawers, swapping out plastic for stainless steel and glass containers, it was time to say farewell to plastic in other areas of my kitchen, like packaging, cleaning tools, and pots and pans. Read on to identify where you can easily begin removing the plastic from your kitchen.

There's Something in the Water

The disposable plastic water bottle scourge of our modern times helped kickstart the plastic waste debate. Thankfully, it's now common to see people walking around with their reusable water bottles, and the San Francisco International Airport has even banned the sale of plastic water bottles in its terminals.

But what about in our homes? What is the best way to provide clean, delicious tasting water to our families without involving plastic?

Often unfiltered tap water is good enough, but sometimes chlorine or ground water minerals that are safe but not tasty can tarnish the flavor of tap water. I like to use activated charcoal sticks as a "back to the future" solution for purifying our water. You can buy charcoal sticks, also known as binchotan charcoal, online or if you live near a Japantown, some stores will carry them in bulk at a cheaper price. Boil one charcoal stick and place it in a glass carafe filled with water. The incredibly porous surface attracts contaminants and leaves you with great-tasting water. There are also now several glass carafe water filter systems on the market so you can skip the more popular plastic containers.

If you love sparkling water (and who doesn't, these days?), how about making your own at home instead of buying individual plastic bottles at huge mark-ups? Your own at-home carbonation system allows you to forgo the plastic waste and save money in the long run.

Bye-Bye, Plastic Containers

With so many alternatives to plastic coming to market, it can be hard to keep everything straight. I recommend steering clear of kitchen tools and cutlery made from bioplastics and molded bamboo even though they're labeled as eco-friendly.

Bioplastics are touted as superior to regular plastic because they're made from plants like tapioca root, sugarcane, and cornstarch, and are considered biodegradable. You've probably seen single-use utensils and cups made from bioplastics hanging out in the aisles with their plastic cousins. But here's the thing: Once these bioplastics end up in a dark compost bin or lost in the environment away from prying eyes, they rarely break down as advertised, according to the Earth Institute at Columbia University.

"While the biodegradability of bioplastics is an advantage, most need high temperature industrial composting facilities to break down and very few cities have the infrastructure needed to deal with them. As a result, bioplastics often end up in land-fills where, deprived of oxygen, they may release methane, a greenhouse gas 23 times more potent than carbon dioxide."[1]

Until bioplastic-derived products improve or commercial systems for their disposal are devel-oped, they should be avoided.

You may also have been confused to run across so many cute kitchen tools made from molded bamboo composite materials marketed as green alternatives. Spatulas, ladles, turners, mixing bowls, measuring cups and are widely available in brightly lacquered finishes. But these also can't be recycled or composted. At end of their life, they're destined for the landfill.

My research shows it's definitely better to choose wooden or bamboo kitchen utensils finished with an organic oil—not the plastic polyurethane lacquer generally used with the composite products. Unlike their colorful cousins made from composite bamboo, they're completely non-toxic and biodegradable.

When it comes to selecting plastic-free container options, I believe the simpler the better. Look to the past for inspiration, starting with glass and steel. Of the plastic substitutes, silicone is currently the best option available. It's a great alternative to plastic lids for leak-proof performance.

Silicone is made from silica that is found in sand. It lasts much longer than plastic and can withstand extreme changes in temperature so if it's lost in the environment, it won't break into smaller pieces and accumulate within living organisms like plastic. In more good news for silicone, if disposed of at a landfill for incineration it converts back into inorganic, harmless ingredients: amorphous silica, carbon dioxide, and water vapor. But be cautious when searching for silicone materials. To save money, many producers mix silicone with plastic or use fillers in their silicone composition. You can identify low-quality silicone when white will show through if you twist or stretch it.

Once you've replaced your old plastic containers in favor of better choices that are healthy for people and the planet, what should you do with them? Instead of just tossing them in the trash, you can extend their use in your office, garage, art room, or bathroom. Repurpose them into storage containers for stationery and other small items. Place one in your bathroom as a mini compost collector or repurpose them as indoor plant containers by poking a few holes in the bottoms for drainage. Let your imagination guide you.

BYOC (Bring Your Own Container)

Purchasing Bulk Items

One of my favorite tactics for reducing packaging waste in the kitchen is to shop in bulk with my own plastic-free containers and bags. I head to the part of the grocery where nuts, candies, granola, flours, and other staples are sold in big bins. I scoop what I need into my containers, mark down on pieces of tape provided by the store the item numbers for the food I've selected, and head to check-out. BYO bags and containers are such an easy way to forgo the plastic and kraft paper bags with plastic windows (not recyclable since they're mixed material) commonly provided near the bulk bins. Adding to the fun, when you get home you'll notice your pantry looks chic with all the glass jars and metal tins.

Buying in bulk is easy to do with any container as long as you know the weight. Some containers, like my company's Blue Water Bentos, have their tare weight printed on the bottom. You can also stock up on reusable cotton produce bags and glass jars with tare weights that work well for wet items like meat and oils. Wondering how tare weights work? By knowing the weight of the container, the cashier can ring you up so you're only paying for the weight of the dry goods, fruit, or other product you're buying. Essentially, they're subtracting the weight of the container or bag from your charge.

If your containers or bags don't have printed weights, stop by the customer service desk and ask a clerk to "tare" it. They will weigh the container, mark the weight on a piece of tape, and stick it to the container for when the cashier rings you up.

Buying Bread

Bread is often sold at grocery stores in plastic sacks or in paper sacks with plastic windows. Apparently bread merchandisers think you need a window to see your bread before purchasing it but did you know the plastic window makes the paper part of the bag unrecyclable? Instead, bring your own reusable bag to tote your bread home, like a waxed cotton bread bag or a pillowcase. Once you are home, simply tuck your wrapped-up loaf in a bread box, like our grandparents did, away from heat and sunlight to keep it fresh. Made of wood, bamboo or metal, back-to-the future bread boxes are widely for sale.

Shopping Small and Local

If you cannot find what you need in bulk at your local natural grocery store, locate a small, local bakery, butcher, or other supplier. Some communities still have old-fashioned milkmen who will deliver milks, cheeses, and other dairy items in reusable containers directly to your home.

Gourmet food bars that offer pre-packaged tubs of olives, salads, cheeses, and other prepared foods will often sell to you in bulk sans packaging if you bring your own container. The same goes for other food items typically sold pre-packaged like ice cream. Ask your local creamery to pack your ice cream in a container you bring.

Food safety laws throughout the United States are changing. In the recent past many grocery stores and restaurants were unwilling to send out their food in the customer's container for fear of running up against local health inspectors who enforced cross contamination codes. This is often no longer the case. For example: in California, new policies were passed in 2019 freeing up reusable shopping practices. So if you've been denied in the past, now is the time to ask again if you can use your own containers to purchase food items.

Tea Without the Teabag

There's nothing like curling up with a good book, or streaming a good movie. A cup of hot tea really adds to the coziness, but if you're not careful in selecting your bagged tea, you could be inadvertently drinking microplastics.

Skip premium tea bags made of polyethylene terephthalate (PET) plastic and nylon. These can release unhealthy microplastics when steeped in nearly boiling water. Instead buy organic tea in bulk and use a metal infuser or strainer. You can easily store the tea in a stainless steel container. For frequent tea sippers looking for something easy, pick up a reusable glass or metal tea thermos with a built-in infuser.

Swap Tip: Best Packaging Practices

If you do need to buy something pre-packaged, like broth, spaghetti sauce, nut milks, baby food purees, and tuna, try to buy brands packaged in glass jars or aluminum cans—never in Tetra Paks (those cartons that look like cardboard on the outside and are lined with foil on the inside). Tetra Paks might look metallic, but don't be fooled. They're not recyclable no matter how much they claim to be. It's too many materials all stuck together (paper, plastic, metal, and on and on). Glass and aluminum, however, are infinitely and easily recyclable.

There is simply no reason to come home from the grocery store burdened with a pile of plastic waste—and definitely no reason to wrap them up in more plastic once you get home. Speaking of which...

No More Plastic Wrap

It's time to turn over a new leaf and ditch the saran wrap. No one likes food waste, but wrapping food in plastic is a poor choice for people and the planet. The cheap plastic film has a bad reputation for leaching estrogen-mimicking toxins like phthalates into food.[1] To make matters worse, this single-use plastic product isn't recyclable. Millions of tons of the wrap head straight for the landfill or incinerator every year.[2]

Fresh palm and banana leaves have served as biodegradable food wraps for generations, but if that's not available to you, read on for a few more options.

There was a time before plastic wrap. Wax paper was used decades before plastic wrap. But don't be fooled! Unfortunately, wax paper today is not actually paper coated in wax—it's paper covered in a thin coat of paraffin, which is a petroleum-based, plastic-related product that is not recyclable. Instead, look for paper coated in beeswax. The practice of oiling parchment or paper has been around since the middle ages. You can be sure that organic paper or cotton coated in natural substances like beeswax, jojoba oil, and tree resin is safe for you, your family, and the environment.

Parchment paper made from unbleached paper certified by the Forest Stewardship Council (FSC), however, is also a good recyclable alternative. It is coated with a very thin layer of non-toxic and biodegradable silicone. Silicone is derived from silicon, which is abundant in nature and non-toxic. Meanwhile, aluminum foil is a viable traditional option to use as an occasional swap for saran wrap since it can be infinitely recycled—just make sure to clean it first before you discard of it in your recycling bin.

Looking for a more novel option? Try adding a filter to your refrigerator to absorb the ethylene gas that triggers fruit ripening and decay. It will help keep your fruits and vegetables fresh for longer without plastic. New products like silicone caps for your cucumber ends, bananas, avocados, and silicone lids for your containers are also clever swaps for plastic wrap.

Sponge Away Plastic

Plastic lurks everywhere in the kitchen, often hidden in plain sight. Let's start with the countertop. Most everyday sponges are derived from polyurethane, an oil-based plastic. Once they're too gross to keep using, they're fit only for the trash can. The same is true for the packaging they're sold in. To add insult to injury, sponges that promise antibacterial or odor-removing benefits are themselves *loaded* with toxic chemicals, including triclosan—an antimicrobial agent (and pesticide) that has been linked to cancer, developmental toxicity, and skin irritation. This chemical has made its way into 60 percent of American waterways, wreaking havoc on marine life.

How about swapping out conventional plastic sponges with biodegradable alternatives? You can find a sponge made from cellulose, a wood pulp product. If you like having a sponge with a scrubber, there are cellulose options with natural loofah stitched on one side for extra dirty pots and pans. The key is to get an alternative that can go directly into your green bin for commercial composting when you're finished with it. If you're a home composter, cutting your biodegradable sponge into small pieces to speed its breakdown may be an option but check with the manufacturer first.

All by itself natural loofah, is another great sponge and scrubber option that's easy to find online. Used for generations by indigenous communities, it's actually a fruit that can grow very large and is processed to remove everything except the network of fibers. We have a chunk of loofah that we purchased at a produce market in San Francisco's Chinatown and have found it to be a great all-purpose tool. It works great for sloughing off dry skin in the bath, too.

Last but not least, good ol' rags are a great scrubbing option and classic back-to-the-future solution. They can offer just as much cleaning power as sponges minus the waste and you can create them for free from old T-shirts, towels, or other scrap cloth you have on hand. But even if you have to purchase rags, they'll last a whole heck of a lot longer and be a whole lot better for your family and for the environment than a plastic sponge.

Soup's On!

The easy-to-clean pots and pans in your kitchen are a prime example of modern technology that results in environmental and health headaches in the long run.

Teflon, which everyone was raving about only a few years ago, is made of polytetrafluoroethylene (PTFE). To make PTFE you need perfluorooctanoic acid (also known as PFOA and C8). Now here's the problem: PFOA can remain in the body for long periods of time and lead to increased cholesterol, harmful effects to a developing fetus or breast-feeding infant, low infant birth weights, and effects on the immune system, liver, and thyroid, according to the U.S. National Library of Medicine.[4]

That doesn't sound so appetizing, does it?

My favorite alternative to non-stick pots and pans is the classic cast iron skillet our grandparents used. This amazing object can last just about forever under the right care. After you purchase yours (or buy it used) read up on seasoning and management to avoid rusting of the cast iron. Pans made of ceramics and stainless steel are great alternatives!

Goodbye Plastic
Personal Challenge

What one thing can I commit to that will reduce my use of plastic in the kitchen?

Example: I will begin shopping from the bulk food sections of my local grocery store with my plastic-free containers in hand.

When you shop in bulk, you are using your pocketbook to send a message to your local grocery store that you're in the market for plastic-free options. If you see holes in their bulk offerings, talk to the management and ask them for improvements.

Citizen Activist Challenge

Already a bulk shopping pro? Spread the plastic-free love! Teach friends and neighbors how to shop in bulk by holding a how-to clinic at a local market. Bring your food containers, bags, and jars and walk them through the process of filling, labeling, and checking out.

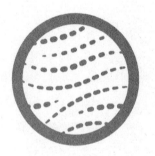

Bathroom

They say beauty is pain, which is quite true for the environment. All that stubborn packaging in the bathroom felt impossible to avoid for a long time.

It was only a few years ago when ditching plastics in the bathroom meant you had to be a DIY heroine, whipping up your own deodorant. I didn't have time for that, so I found some local makers and would order their eco products, specifically requesting tin, glass or cardboard packaging. Now, earth-friendly (and effective) toiletries are widely available online and new solutions are popping up all the time!

I get bubbly talking about the fun I've had giving all the plastic bottles in my shower the boot (we used up the contents first and recycled the bottles). I've moved our family over to using a corrugated birch soap tray bedecked with a colorful variety of barred soaps, conditioners and shampoos. Instead of being sullen mildew-collectors in the corner of my shower shelf, my bottle-less products now look like a rainbow of French macarons elegantly on display. And it's completely effortless to achieve this in your own home too.

There is an exciting variety of green products like solid shampoos, conditioners, body lotions, and even toothpaste (chewable tabs) all sold in plastic-free packaging, available online or in eco-friendly stores. And we know the tide is changing when squeezable products like lip balm, sunscreen, and toothpaste are available in metal tins and cardboard tubes. Whatever you are looking for, it's becoming easier and easier to find a plastic-free option.

Returning to some older practices like metal razors and tooth tabs or powders can also help save the planet and our bank accounts. Try to recall what your parents and grandparents used for personal care and you'll be on the right track.

Bulk shopping is expanding from the grocery to the realm of personal care. Just search online for "zero waste bulk stores" in local directories and bring your containers to fill up. Look good and do good.

Brush (Plastic-Free) Twice a Day

Bamboo is a trendy material these days and with good reason. It can be shaped into toothbrushes, soap dishes, cosmetic cases and other everyday items typically made from plastic, and it's fast growing, oxygen producing, and 100% biodegradable. But don't be fooled by composite bamboo that's ground up and molded with polymers because this won't biodegrade. (See page 61 for more cautionary information about composite bamboo material.)

In the past few years, I've found hundreds of plastic toothbrushes during my beach clean-ups. Did you know that a billion toothbrushes are thrown away every year in the United States alone? They're all but impossible to recycle since they are made from assorted types of plastics and not accepted by recycling collectors. Got old extras lying around the house? Use for cleaning or crafts before tossing in the trash.

Bamboo toothbrushes are a huge improvement over their plastic counterparts and with several brands on the market and no downgrade in effectiveness or convenience, it's easy to make the switch. A few even have biodegradable bristles, but most bristles are still made from nylon, so you'll need to snap the head off to discard it before composting the bamboo handle.

Toothpaste producers have also been getting a bit creative with plastic-free options like chewable neem plant sticks, tooth powders, organic pastes sold in small glass jars and chewable tablets. If you go the tooth powder route, make sure it's free of the tiny, scrubbing pieces of plastic called microbeads. These slip through wastewater processing systems and into our oceans. They are mistaken for food by marine animals, and contribute to starvation and bioaccumulation.

In India and other countries, sticks from the neem tree have been used to prevent cavities and gum disease for centuries. Chew on the stick a little to get the fibers to fray and rub the bristles along your teeth and gums. Trim and repeat. Compost when used up. This all-natural, completely biodegradable option is readily available for purchase online and in stores.

And last but not least: dental floss. Regular dental floss is made of waxed nylon, a form of plastic. Instead, look for floss that is made of materials like silk that naturally decompose. Some plastic-free brands even come coated in beeswax for easy gliding between teeth. You'll find these options widely sold online and in natural apothecaries in plastic-free refillable glass vials as well as recyclable cardboard boxes.

Many plastic-free dental products come in reusable glass jars with a bamboo spatula for application or are shipped in compostable craft paper boxes with biodegradable vegetable ink labeling. In addition to their many environmental upsides, these plastic-free options are also less toxic to humans since they're usually free of fluoride, parabens, fillers, flavoring, and preservatives.

Swap Tip: Pocket-Friendly

Shaving can be a real drag on your body, your wallet, and the environment. Disposable plastic razors are just that, disposable. Besides providing plenty of fodder for landfills, they're overpriced, especially for women. Turn back the clock (and pad your wallet) by using an old school metal safety razor and mug soap instead of a disposable one paired with chemical-laden aerosol shaving foam. For both guys and gals, switching over to the eco-friendly, plastic-free option will net you a closer, more comfortable and more affordable shave. Safety razor blades can be purchased for replacement at a fraction of the cost of those throw-away plastic heads with three and five blades and you'll be helping say goodbye to the disposal of two billion plastic razors each year in the United States.

Roll Up or Down
The Eco Way

We all need toilet paper. But we don't need to buy it in cases and packs wrapped up tight in plastic. It's a mess, but for a long time I didn't know my plastic-free options and I kept picking up conventional toilet paper at local big box retailers. You might need to order online, but it's entirely possible to ditch the plastic-wrapped rolls and switch to fully recycled and unbleached toilet paper sold either unwrapped by office and restaurant suppliers or individually wrapped in tissue paper and packed in cardboard cartons.

That's a wrap, folks!

Ladies, Get in Formation

Innovations in feminine care have really picked up in recent years, but most ladies still don't know all the options available to them. Traditional pads and tampons are not the answer anymore (if they ever were).

A woman uses more than 10,000 pads and tampons in her lifetime, so swapping these products out for natural, biodegradable products is a great way to say goodbye to plastic. Conventional pads and tampons are partially made from plastic and are neither compostable nor biodegradable. In fact, menstrual products are one of the most common items found in beach clean-ups.

Plastic tampon applicators are known colloquially as "beach whistles" among litter collectors. While organic, chlorine-free tampons and pads are better alternatives than their traditional counterparts, they still end up in the landfill or ocean. They simply aren't as sanitary and safe as plastic-free options like silicone cups, natural sponges, and ultra-absorbent panties. While some of these may take some getting used to, plenty of women love these new ways of taking control of their periods.

Sea sponge is a natural and renewable material that has been used by women for ages as a tampon alternative. They're comfortable and environmentally friendly. Sponges easily regrow once harvested so there's no need to worry about them being overfarmed.

Silicone cups are safe, clean, and will save you money in the long run. A cup can last up to 10 years if cared for correctly. Another option is washable menstrual panties that replace pads, tampons, liners and cups or serve as extra protection.

Goodbye Plastic
Personal Challenge

What one thing can I commit to that will reduce my use of plastic in the bathroom?

Example: I will begin buying recycled toilet paper packaged in paper, not plastic.

Pro tip: Buy paper-packaged toilet paper in bulk from your local restaurant and hotel supply store to save big.

Citizen Activist Challenge

Talk to your dentist about the plastic crisis and how toothbrush disposal is creating a major problem for the environment. Suggest a bamboo toothbrush alternative for giveaway in their office. Recommend other giveaways that are plastic-free.

Bedroom

A good night's rest can make a big difference. Everything from our mood to our weight is affected by how well we sleep, so it's no surprise that we are always on the lookout for ways to catch better ZZZs.

Hopefully, we're all spending seven hours or more in our beds every day, which makes it a really important area in which to make the best healthy and environmentally safe choices we can. Restful ZZZs are a healthy habit, but you definitely want to avoid PVCs, PBDEs, CH2O, BZ and many other plastic chemicals known by their acronyms that are likely to be lurking in your bedroom.

Unfortunately, I was asleep at the wheel when it came to tackling my bedroom. In fact, I'm still working on upgrading this room. Like many of you, I started my own eco-journey in the kitchen but I've since learned there is plenty of plastic to tackle in my bedroom. It has reminded me that being a steward for the environment isn't just about buying reusable containers and avoiding straws. While those actions are important, it takes so much more to overhaul your dependence on plastic in all the overlooked nooks and crannies of life.

With some creative thinking, a bit of research, and a little more time, we can transform our bedrooms into sustainable and healthy oases. I start with the cheapest and easiest at the top and progress to other more challenging and expensive swaps, like selecting a plastic-free bed.

Fan the (Non-Toxic) Flames

I enjoy unwinding by candlelight. I even have a small table in my room where I regularly burn candles. But while paraffin candles may look innocent, inside their soft glow they contain petroleum and often unhealthy fragrances. Additionally, finding a candle that's not sold in plastic packaging can be tough.

Paraffin is a petroleum-derived product that , like plastic, you shouldn't be breathing. Paraffin candles can release known carcinogens like benzene (BZ) and toluene, and can even contain heavy metals like lead in their wicks. The fragrance in candles typically uses a chemical found in plastics called phthalate, which is an estrogen-mimicker. Even a few hours of burning can create dangerous levels of airborne heavy metals. Combine the off gassing of the burning petroleum wax with synthetic fragrances and you've got a toxic combination.

Luckily, beeswax candles are a safe alternative. They burn with almost no smoke or scent and clean the air by releasing negative ions that bind with toxins. Doesn't that make you breathe easier? Other safe alternatives include palm and soy wax candles and votives sold in stores and online in cardboard boxes.

Plastic-Free Pillow Talk

Most beds are doused with fire-retardant chemicals and covered in plastic mattress covers, but completely overhauling your bed can take time and money. Luckily, there are some smaller fixes you can make as you start out on your plastic-free quest—like changing your pillows.

Do you know what lurks inside your pillows? It's probably a plastic down alternative like small curled polyester bits that have been heated and forced through spinnerets into fiber.

How about replacing your down alternative pillow with a recycled version, for example, pillows stuffed with polyester made from 100% recyclable plastic bottles (about 17 per pillow according to manufacturers)? If you prefer the classic feel of feathers, consider purchasing pillows made with extras from poultry farms so no chickens are harmed in the making of your pillows. If you like memory foam, try a buckwheat pillow instead. Birch fiber and recycled cotton are other plastic-free options that don't harm the planet. With all of these choices, it's not too difficult to make the bed of your eco-friendly dreams.

Pillows need to be replaced every two to three years and at the end of their lives, most end up as landfill. Because of sanitary concerns, they can't be donated. If you have a pup, considering gifting your old pillows to them. No pets? Try local pet shelters or friends instead.

Read All About It

If you're like me, you always end up with a stack of magazines and books taking up space on your nightstand. For a plastic-free alternative to plastic bins opt for natural willow or wicker baskets. They always look one-of-a-kind. The same is true when it comes to shoe caddies and under-bed storage. Options made from biodegradable natural materials are easily available online or at local marketplaces. They make great gifts as well.

Here's a tip: when spring cleaning comes around, you can easily recycle glossy magazines and books—even hardcovers with the cover ripped off. Of course, it's also a good idea to donate books to charity or your local library if they'll accept them. Some libraries even have a second-hand store where they sell donated books to help support library programs.

Swap Tip: Pretty as a Picture

As a former journalist, I love to document my life. From pictures taken for the newspaper assignments of my youth to our family vacations today, I'm always snapping photos. You will find picture frames throughout my house; I make sure I'm using the most eco-friendly ones.

Turn your attention to the materials you're using in your home. Many frames are made from cheap plastic molded to look like wood which can't be recycled. If there's a number on the frame, you can search for a location in your area that accepts that type of plastic, but facilities typically only accept and sort beverage bottles that have value in the overseas resale markets. I prefer reusing old wooden frames, picking up second-hand frames at garage sales or thrift shops. As a last resort, I will buy new ones made of natural, biodegradable materials.

Choosing Good Bedfellows

Let's talk about the elephant in your bedroom: your mattress. Most mattresses are made from various plasticky petrochemicals, and recycling them is tricky. So before buying a new one, it's wise to find one that's non-toxic.

I learned the hard way that mattresses can create air quality issues. Today's ubiquitous memory foam mattresses are made from polyurethane, a type of plastic that often contains chemicals like formaldehyde (CH_2O). A few years ago, we bought my daughter one that was labelled "low VOC," but even so it stunk up her room with worrisome plasticky fumes.

If you love the feel of a foam mattress, natural latex is a popular alternative. Or you can go foam-free with a mattress made from cotton and wool. You might think that your foam mattress is older and has already off-gassed, so it's ok to use. Unfortunately this isn't true. Foam degrades with age and continues to release hormone-disrupting chemicals, like the fire retardant PBDE (polybrominated diphenyl ethers), into your bedroom over time. These chemicals are accumulating in humans and wildlife at alarming levels.[1]

As you probably know, buying a new mattress is a big investment. Before taking that plunge start by looking into your options. Traditional mattresses are tough to recycle because they're made out of a variety of materials, like springs and wood, and need to be taken apart first. This can be a bit of a challenge but well worth the reward to some recyclers. If your current mattress is foam, many recyclers are finding ways to breathe new life into the petrochemical material by down-cycling the foam into things like carpet padding.

This planning process might take some time, so see if you can refresh your current one with a plastic-free mattress cover, pillow top, or other alternative. These protectors can offer odor and wetness protection as well as an extra layer of comfort and support.

Be aware that many mattress protectors are made from plastic, including off-gassing vinyl and other varieties that are especially toxic. That's not what we need for a good night's sleep. Find companies that make pads or protectors out of sustainable and non-toxic materials and sleep easy, knowing you eliminated unhealthy materials from your sleeping quarters.

Made to Last

One of my most interesting discoveries on my path to a plastic-free life was that our elders had the right idea when it comes to sustainable objects. For example, we still have furniture in my house passed down from my grandparents, while the pressed particle board items haven't lasted more than a couple years. So when you're thinking about what kind of bed frame to purchase, consider a solid wood piece that can be refinished over and over again.

Did you know that metal bed frames and other metal furniture are also easily recycled? You can either resell them online or take them to a scrap metal yard. You may even make some extra cash!

Goodbye Plastic Personal Challenge

What one thing can I commit to that will reduce my use of plastic in the bedroom?

Example: I will only purchase soy or beeswax candles that do not come in plastic packaging from now on.

Or: I will start small by swapping plastic accessories in my bedroom for natural ones while researching mattress replacements and setting a budget.

Citizen Activist Challenge

The next time you need to buy a housewarming gift for a friend, get them a soy or beeswax candle and let them know about the health and environmental hazards of paraffin candles.

Or: Find local resources for mattress recycling and draft a post for your local online neighborhood message board to let your community know why it's important to recycle rather than landfill these bedroom beasts.

Dining Room & Entertaining

Saying goodbye to plastic in the dining room was my easiest space. After all, most of us already have reusable dining ware made out of sustainable materials like ceramic, glass, and stainless steel. With some light weeding of plasticky outdoor dining plates, platters, cups and decorations, you're on your way! So if you're looking for quick satisfaction, start your plastic-free journey in the dining room.

What was more difficult for me was entertaining, especially when it came to outdoor events. I dreaded the dozens of dishes piling up in my kitchen, and finding non-breakable, plastic-free, and reusable plates seemed like an impossible task…until I cracked the code.

Now, let me save you some time and trouble with my top tips for throwing fun, stress-free, and (nearly) plastic-free shindig in your dining room, your garden, at school, your office or anywhere!

Put It In the Invitation

Set yourself up for success by being honest and letting people know it's a plastic-free party. If you need people to bring their own reusable containers, ask them up front. If it's a potluck, request items in reusable containers instead of plastic throwaways. Don't expect people to share your values without any notice. Making an announcement is an easy way to invite participation.

Ask For Help

Once everyone arrives, you can also make a short announcement about what you're doing and why. Ask your guests for their help in reaching your goal of a plastic-free party. Let them know where the compost and recycling bins are located. Invite people to make themselves at home and use your kitchen sink if they have reusable serving platters or other items they've brought that need a quick wash before being toted home.

Build Your Stash

If you throw a lot of parties and you have the storage space, it's worth investing in enough dishes, glasses, and utensils for your parties so you never have to resort to single-use plastic items. Put out a call for items from people on your neighborhood online bulletin board or purchase what you can at a thrift store.

I've picked up mixed utensils at garage sales and thrift stores over the years and store them in a caddy with a carrying handle. For glasses I have various sizes and shapes of mason jars, including tiny ones that work great as wine glasses for outdoor entertaining.

For very large events and when reusables are not practical, I find certified compostable options, like bamboo plates without plastic lacquers. Paper plates coated with water-resistant plastic are not compostable or recyclable, so don't let the word "paper" on the packaging fool you. And remember: Anything tainted with food grease or scraps, like a pizza box, cannot be recycled and must be composted.

BYOE (Bring Your Own *Everything*)

If you don't have enough of your own reusable dinner supplies yet, you can always ask your guests to join in on the plastic-free fun by bringing their own. When I first started throwing plastic-free parties, I would ask people to bring their own utensils and cups. The upside: everyone washed their own dishes before taking them back home so I didn't have to!

Don't Do Dishes Yourself

Ensuring everything is reusable does mean a lot more dishes to wash, but it's a small price to pay for a truly sustainable party.

If your guests aren't proactively asking to help, feel free to ask them. If it means making our future a little greener, I'm sure they'll say yes. My close friends are always happy to lend a hand in exchange for delicious food and even better company. For really big events, I hire teens from the neighborhood to take charge of clean-up so I'm free to mingle.

Another good tip to cut down on washing up is to skip the trays and serve everything straight from the pot.

Smart Hydration

Everyone is obsessed with sparkling water these days—and that means way more plastic bottle waste. Ask yourself: is a little bit of the bubbly truly worth it?

If you're not equipped to make sparkling water at home (see the Kitchen chapter for how-to options), skip it. Serve filtered tap water with lemon, mint, cucumbers, or a variety of herbs and fruit instead.

I've picked up a couple of glass drink dispensers with spigots that sit side by side on a metal stand. I usually make iced tea with plastic-free tea bags for one side and something like infused water or lemonade for the other.

Hide the Trash Can

I like to only have labelled bins for recyclables and compost items out during parties—no landfill. It's a pretty effective trick to slyly move guests into the direction of reusable and compostable items.

Eco Decorating

I hate to burst your bubble but balloons and their strings can entangle, choke, and kill marine life and other animals when lost in the environment. Some balloons are made of latex, which is considered a biodegradable material, but one which takes months or years to break down and until then, is hazardous to wildlife. And don't be fooled by the shiny balloons that look like they're made out of metal. They're actually Mylar plastic coated with shiny metal-like colors or foil and are not bio-degradable or recyclable.

Forego disposable streamers made from plastic or throw-away paper for festive, reusable artisan banners made out of cotton pennants with designs and words. When I was in India recently I picked up a couple of lovely knitted pennants in bright blues and golds with pom poms that I plan to use and reuse at my upcoming events.

Swap Tip: Eco-Friendly Furbishing

Decorating with found items in nature, whether it's roadside wildflowers or autumn leaves, is a lovely way to bring the season into your home. Next time, ditch the disposable decor and look out your window for inspiration.

You Can't Control Everything

Inevitably, people are going to bring stuff that turns into trash. When a guest shows up with a plastic platter of veggies just smile and thank them. It might be hard to bite your tongue, but try to lead by example instead. Invite them warmly into the plastic-free lifestyle; don't chase them out with a snarky attitude or educational criticism.

Goodbye Plastic Personal Challenge

What one thing can I commit to that will reduce my use of plastic at parties?

Example: I will no longer buy single-use plastic items like cups, plates, utensils, and decorations.

If you want to go a step further, try making everything you provide as a host be compostable or reusable, such as cloth napkins, ceramic dishes, and glassware.

Citizen Activist Challenge

Host a neighborhood plastic-free block party that spreads the message about plastic pollution and the ways we can reduce plastic waste. If you're ready to take on an even bigger challenge, ask your school, church, or other community group if you can take the lead with making their next event plastic-free.

Office &
School

Whether I'm working from home or commuting to the office, I've discovered many strategies to dramatically cut down my plastic use. It takes a little work to rejigger your office toolkit and ditch needless plastic, but I know from experience that once upgrades are in place, you'll find it easy to keep up a plastic-free office lifestyle. You'll enjoy less clutter too!. I've worked hard to develop plastic-free best practices for my own work life, and I hope by sharing these tips, I can help you bid farewell to plastic in your work and at school.

Put Your Money Where Your Plastic Isn't

Office and school supplies are a great place to start reducing your plastic use. Many common items are now being made from recyclable and sustainable materials instead of plastic such as windowless mailing envelopes, craft paper packing tape, and wooden pencils to replace markers.

Before you buy any new office or school supplies, do the research to find suppliers specializing in eco-friendly products made by ethical companies. These retailers have researched extensively to build an assortment of plastic-free and plastic-light options, so you can get everything you need in one place.

Pay special attention to any new-to-market businesses who might be working to develop innovative, zero-waste recyclable office solutions. These may include plastic-free white board crayons made from wood; highlighter pens (that are actually wooden pencils); notebooks made from reusable whiteboard-style folios; and even staplers that clip papers together without any staples, such that the discarded paper can be easily recycled. By searching out those companies that are an active part of the plastic-free movement and supporting them with your purchases, you not only lead by example but speak with your spending!

Plastic-free electronics accessories like bamboo phone stands and cotton twill computer sleeves are available on maker marketplaces. If you look around, you'll find oodles of refillable replacements for what were once one-off items like ballpoint pens, whiteboard markers, and laser printer cartridges.

Turn back the clock and get yourself a metal or wooden refillable fountain pen. Or skip paper all together and go with a digital notebook where you can save your scribbles to the cloud with an app. While you may not be able to get away entirely from plastic, you can at least switch to reusable materials to cut down on waste.

The more you buy, the more these eco-manufacturers will thrive and bring to market game-changing products to help further reduce our dependence on plastic.

Eat Lunch, Not Plastic

When you're at work or school you need fuel, but it's possible to avoid plastic in the process. Whether getting take-out or bringing your lunch to work every day, reusable, plastic-free containers and utensils are the best way to cut down on needless waste. Seeing your plastic-free lunches may even encourage those around you to practice similar eco-friendly meals.

Ask your company to provide a budget to replace plastic throwaway cups, plates, utensils, glasses, and mugs at the office, or request a filter on the tap water faucet to encourage people to stop bringing plastic bottles. If they won't fund these eco-friendly switches, think about starting a trend to bring reusable cups, bowls, plates, and utensils to the office to share.

In the Dining Room & Entertaining chapter I discussed how to throw a plastic-free party. How about throwing one with your coworkers or schoolmates? Work together to buy sets of reusable items for everyone to use, or have everyone bring their extras from home. Add additional signage to make it easy to recycle and compost. It's always more fun to tackle these issues with a community.

Reuse Like Your Grandpa Did

Instead of throwing away the things you're not currently using, save them for future reuse. My grandparents made an artform out of reusing. A meticulously organized and sorted corner of their garage was dedicated to items waiting to be reused. Reusing things is a good way to help the environment, especially if you have a build-up of plastic items like binders and containers. Please don't throw them away; simply recycle the old contents and store them for later use. Other great office and school supplies to keep on hand are white boards and broken crayons. Some of these items can even be repurposed for homemade holiday cards, truly giving meaning to reuse as an artform.

Here are some fun and easy ways to give new life to old items instead of buying new plastic ones:

- **Ripped binders:** Buy some colorful, nontoxic tape to patch them together.
- **Notebooks:** Rip out the used paper in your notebooks and use the rest.
- **Backpacks:** Wash, repair, and re-stitch (maybe with a fun new patch).

Even if you can't find another use for your plastic castaways or you're cramped for space, I bet someone else can. Consider offering them up on an online neighborhood, school, or work forum to see who else may need them. Bonus: when it's your turn to need something, you're sure to find someone on that forum happy to give it away.

Goodbye Plasticky Junk Mail

Offices create a lot of waste and a main culprit is plastic junk mail. Have you ever noticed how much plastic enters the home through the mailbox?

It's easy to reduce your plastic and paper footprint by unsubscribing from junk mailing lists, credit card offers (which often include a free, fake plastic card), cancelling unwanted catalogs and magazines (which can include cosmetic product samples in plastic pouches) and switching to e-billing for all bills so you stop getting envelopes with plastic windows that aren't recyclable.

To learn how to register your address and opt-out of junk mailings, see the Resources section at the back of the book.

Don't Forget to Recycle At Work

If your office or school doesn't have one already, you can work towards implementing a recycling policy for things such as plastics, paper, CDs, batteries, pens, and business cards. Create awareness about what can be recycled and how. While it's standard practice at home, many offices don't recycle yet.

Goodbye Plastic Personal Challenge

What one thing can I commit to that will reduce my use of plastic at my place of work or study?

Example: I will only purchase recyclable office supplies from green-certified vendors.

I will refuse freebie pens" to "Or: I will refuse freebie pens

Citizen Activist Challenge

There are lots of ways to help your company or school say goodbye to plastic. Make the business case to your office or school manager about replacing disposable items in the kitchen with eco-friendly reusable ones. Chances are making the switch will have long-term cost-savings for them.

You can also lobby to remove vending machines that sell snacks in single-use containers.

Closet &
Clothing

Once I turned my kitchen and bathroom around, I started looking at other rooms in my house and things that I use every day. Of course, clothing was at the top of the list. I'm the kind of person who wears things past their expiration date, leaving them unfit for charity.

I started thinking more acutely about each piece, noticing that many of the fabrics I wear are synthetic, not compostable, and not really recyclable. Textile waste is often overlooked when we think about plastic waste but it's estimated that U.S. consumers throw away about 81 pounds of clothing every year, including large amounts of synthetic textiles made from plastics. Innovations in textile recycling are coming, like melting cottons and polyesters into liquids that are spun into fibers, but recovery rates for textile recycling in the USA are currently only around 15 percent.[1]

Yes, plastic is truly everywhere. Polyester, nylon, and almost all 'vegan leather' are molded from the same base as plastic: petroleum. Production of these fabrics creates a hefty dose of greenhouse gases and they'll take hundreds of years to break down. Even fleece made from recycled plastic bottles is causing problems in the ocean as micro plastics from laundry are released into the waste stream.

Suddenly your closet isn't looking all that nice, is it? For the past several years I've attempted to buy only natural, earth-friendly fabrics and it's not easy. Here are some tips to help you organize your closet with less plastic.

Check the Label

To some, labels are everything. To me, they help me assess my plastic clothing situation. Apparel brands are legally required to disclose the composition of fabrics. Once you know what you're working with, you can start transforming your wardrobe.

Hiding in plain sight: polyester, acrylic, Lycra, nylon, spandex, polyester fleece, elastane, and polyamide. They're all plastic.

There are a few semi-synthetic fabrics made from renewable sources that are more sustainable. Check your tags for: rayon, viscose, Tencel, or modal. These are lightweight, man-made fabrics derived from plants.

Vegan Isn't *Always* the Answer

Any product that is being marketed as a vegan alternative is going to be synthetic. Look for cruelty-free alternatives, such as certified down, regenerative wool, and artisan-made, vegetable-tanned, or upcycled leather products.

Back-to-Nature Fibers

Choose organic cotton, wool, hemp, Tencel (made from sustainable wood pulp), silk, and linen (made from plants) whenever you can. But since natural fibers aren't waterproof, wrinkle-free, ultra-packable, or lightweight, you'll probably miss some functionality like stretching. Knitwear provides some stretch but nothing compares to polyester. Be prepared to compromise and go easy on yourself as you start to transition your wardrobe to plastic-free alternatives. Some of us may never be okay with saggy 100% cotton underwear.

There are plenty of organic cotton options for workout gear, but when it comes to sports bras, yoga pants, and swim wear, you are probably going to want the stretch that comes with synthetics. There are numerous companies that make bathing suits and workout gear out of recycled materials and sustainable fabrics like hemp. You probably won't, however, find anything that's made entirely of natural fibers. For maximum eco-friendliness, secondhand is your best bet.

Invariably, going natural will cause your style to change. Bodycon dresses (a la the Kardashians) will become a thing of your past. On the bright side, the care and attention needed with natural fibers means a more constructed, and often more sophisticated silhouette. And, finally, your body will be able to breathe again! Plus, you'll be using your pocketbook to reduce demand and production of virgin plastic textiles.

Shop Secondhand Thoughtfully

High-performance items like rain jackets, winter puffy coats, and lightweight camping gear will always come in synthetics. The alternative is traditional, heavy, low-performance waxed canvas and shearling that would require you to hire a Sherpa just to go hiking for a weekend.

The answer here is again to buy secondhand gear that is guaranteed to last for a long time and that can be brought back to the retailer for repairs. Buying polyester items from a thrift store is always better than virgin polyester.

The one category in which eco-friendly secondhand excels is denim. You'll find vintage, non-stretch jeans that are entirely cotton in plenty of thrift and consignment stores all over the country.

Vet the Brands

I try to buy second-hand as much as possible, but when I do need to buy new items like underwear, I research brands that are in line with my values. For me, this means small businesses with a sustainable practice that support organic farming and fair trade.

Consider brands that are using recycled plastics or cotton to make their clothing. By using recycled materials, the demand for new plastic is reduced while strengthening the market for used plastic—meaning that it's less likely to go to waste.

Buy Something You'll Actually Wear

Yes, that may sound like a no brainer, but trust me, it's easy to forget. We're all easily swayed by bargains and shiny objects. It's too easy to walk into a store and leave with bags full of cheap clothes from the sale rack.

I've purchased many "bargains" that have sat in my wardrobe, never worn. I used to have a real weakness for price tags telling me something was 70 percent off. When I first started shopping for clothing second-hand, the same thing happened. There were so many great items that were so cheap! I didn't ask myself, "Do I need it? Will I wear it? Is it worth it?" Instead, I'd just think, "Wow, what a bargain!"

Take your time shopping. A bargain is only a bargain if it is something that you'll wear often. Ask yourself if you would buy it at full price. You need to love the item more than the price tag for it to be worth bringing home.

Make a list of key items you determine are worth their price, like a cotton blouse or trench coat. Look for classic pieces, not the latest trends. That pair of Levi's you splurged on will be with you far longer than those skinny jeans with the stretch. Be ruthless on size; if it fits well, you're more likely to wear it. Don't settle for less. Wait until you find the perfect piece for you.

Goodbye (Again) Plastic Packaging

Most stores are fine with your using your own bag or will provide you with a paper bag to carry your purchased goods, but here and there you still have to be assertive in refusing a plastic bag, such as when shopping online. When making a purchase, email your e-retailer to let them know you don't want your clothes sent in a plastic bag.

Some shops are already reusing packaging from their suppliers or wrapping clothes in paper before packaging them in cardboard boxes. The more often you demand plastic-free packaging practices, the more effort online shops will make to adapt.

Get Your Money's Worth

Last note on saying goodbye to plastic in your wardrobe: Going natural doesn't mean you should throw away your plastic garments. Actually, that's maybe the worst thing you could do. Textile waste is so nefarious that polyester donations often wind up in developing countries where they skip the landfill and wind up on streets and clogging drains. Unless they contain unhealthy toxins and must be trashed, keep your older garments and wear them as long as possible. This will be a long process, and that's alright. You might find a cleaning use for cut up synthetic clothing or stuff them in the take-back bin at any retailer that has an in-store recycling program.

Goodbye Plastic Personal Challenge

What one thing can I commit to that will reduce the amount of plastic in my wardrobe?

Example: I will only purchase new items from sustainable, eco-friendly brands that are in line with my values.

Citizen Activist Challenge

If you love certain brands that only use virgin synthetics what can you do? Let them know they'll lose your business if they don't start switching to natural or recycled fibers. It may take more than one customer to call in so ask your friends to help. Every customer who tells them that they would prefer clothing in natural or recycled fibers will help convince them to make the switch.

Laundry Room & Cleaning

The amount of plastic waste and toxins that get tossed into the waste stream during our regular laundry routines is mind-boggling. We think we're cleaning, when actually we're polluting. Microplastics wash off our fleece and other polyester plastic clothing. Plus plastic bottles, tubs and other containers used for detergents, sprays, powders…and all of it are completely unnecessary.

There is some good news, however. When I decided to clean up my act in the laundry room, I was delighted to discover just how many easy swaps and eco-friendly options are available. It's a welcome change—just a couple of years ago, plastic-free consumers would have to make their own products from vinegar and baking soda. (This is still a great option if you're into that kind of thing, by the way, and there are a ton of recipes available online.)

Since there are so many great options available to help you say goodbye to plastic in the laundry room, the trick is actually knowing where and what to cut out and reduce to make your laundry experience more green and more beneficial for both the world and your clothing in the long run.

Day-One Easy Swaps

There are lots of ways to up your eco-game when it comes to your laundry and household cleaning, and the best place to start is also the most obvious: getting rid of plastic containers. When selecting your eco-friendly detergent or cleaning product, whether it's a liquid, spray or power, first check to make sure that it's not packaged in plastic. There are great powder options, for example, that come packaged in a cardboard box and don't contain toxins like phosphates.

On that note, it's also time to ditch the bleach. Bleach typically comes in a plastic bottle, a no-no in itself, and is both terrible for the environment and irritating for your skin. Other prime plastic candidates for replacement include disposable polyester dryer sheets and liquid fabric softeners sold in plastic bottles. These sheets, which cannot be composted or recycled since they're made from plastic polyester material, are coated with synthetic fragrances, contain estrogen-mimicking chemicals, as well as fatty acids that coat the clothing and reduce static.

Some other laundry room eco-tips include:

- Buying dishwasher detergent in bulk through a home delivery subscription service and storing it in refillable tins.

- Ditch those ubiquitous blue rinse aids for your dishwasher. Choose instead a non-toxic alternative that doesn't contain harmful chemicals, which can leach through wastewater treatment plants and contaminate our oceans. It's easy to pick a rinse aid that's ocean-friendly by checking an online directory, like the Environmental Working Group (for more info, see Resources), that third-party verifies product safety.

- Swap out your laundry stain sprays for an old-fashioned stain stick and use a wood handle brush to scrub it into your clothing. Being eco-friendly doesn't mean you can't have clean clothes!

No More Laundry for Lunch

You might not know it, but our laundry and our lunch—or, more broadly, the global food supply—are strongly linked. Every time we do laundry, our clothes (especially fleece) shed tiny plastic microfibers, which then go down the drains of our washing machines, through the wastewater treatment facilities and finally into our waterways. These plastic fibers, primarily polyester in composition, then get ingested by little fish and sea critters which mistake the microplastics for food.

Of course, it doesn't end there. That's just how plastic starts moving up the food chain. Predators, such as large fish, sharks and birds (and humans, too!) then ingest these little sea critters, as well as plants and even sea salt that's been contaminated with microplastics. Over time, the toxins from these microplastics start to bioaccumulate in our systems, leading to deadly health and reproductive problems.

When I came to understand these connections, it struck me how literally everything in this world is connected to everything else, and it redoubled my resolve to remove as much plastic as possible from my cleaning regimen. To help cut down on the release of these harmful microfibers into our wastewater systems, opt for one of the new products available for sale online that help capture these tiny pieces of plastic. These microfiber-catching balls grab the tiny plastic particles during the washing cycle and collect them in little grooves instead of allowing them to pass out the drain. There are also bags available, made from a very fine weave, that allow water to pass inside but blocks the microplastics from escaping, capturing them for disposal.

Using these specialized tools while washing synthetics allows you to remove this contamination before it washes down the drain and dispose of it with the rest of your garbage.

Pods No, Berries Yes!

You might remember the trend of kids popping laundry pods into their mouths to make daring videos from a few years back. While it's 100 percent clear that these colorful blobs of goopy toxins, intended for our dishwashers and laundry, aren't safe to eat. But did you know they're terrible for the environment, too?

At first, these convenient pods seemed non-toxic: the polyvinyl alcohol (PVA) film which encapsulates the detergent inside supposedly dissolves in water, according to the manufacturers. But studies of the particulate matter found in our oceans shows that microplastic PVAs are passing through wastewater plants and are finding their way into our marine systems.

When it comes to pods, the only ones we recommend are grown on trees! Also called soapnuts, these made-by-nature pods are the fruit of the Sapindus Mukorossi tree, which grows in the foothills of the Himalayan mountains. These berries are super useful since they can be used as both a detergent and a fabric softener. The skin of the fruit contains plant saponin, a completely natural and gentle soap that has been used for centuries to clean skin and clothes. Saponin works as a surfactant, breaking the surface tension of the water and creating a lather that lifts dirt and grease from skin, leaving it suspended in the water while it gets rinsed away. For laundry, this surfactant action penetrates the fibers of your clothing, too, lifting stains from the fabric and washing them away with the water.

This is just one example of how nature offers many solutions for modern-day, plastic-free living.

If a material seems too good to be true, it probably is. Find an alternative that's natural until independent studies have definitely shown that the plastic-replacement is safe for people and planet.

Note: While we focused on pods here, anything with scrubbing agents should also be avoided, as these are composed of the same beads banned in cosmetics that end up in the ocean. Look for products with natural materials like ground coconut shells instead.

Less Washing is Best

When you are using a washing machine and dryer, here are a few tips to make things more eco-friendly:

- Wash your polyesters as infrequently as possible to reduce microfiber release into the wastewater stream.
- Warm water uses more electricity and isn't all that good for your clothing anyway: the heat

breaks down fibers more quickly. Since cotton is one of the most toxic crops on earth, we want to make sure to extend its life as much as possible! The same goes for using your dryer at super-hot temperatures.

- Make sure to separate clothing by texture and color.
- Don't overload your machine. Of course, you want to be mindful of wasting water, but overloading a washer can also wear out your clothes—and machine—faster.

Back to the Future

No matter what room you're cleaning up, I find it always helps to think about what your grandparents did. More than likely, the old way was the more eco-friendly option!

Hand-washing and line drying clothes is a prime example. (You knew I was going to suggest this!) It saves so much electricity, and all it costs is a bit of extra prep time. Sweaters, organic cotton, and undergarments all benefit greatly from hand-washing. Just make sure to hang dry or lay flat, depending on the garment. I find it also helps to gently wrap your delicates in a towel to absorb extra water before line drying.

Ahh…Fresh Air

The bathroom is always a challenge when it comes to smell. A lot of bathroom sprays contain harmful, toxic ingredients like phlathetes. Skip this and purchase an all-natural spray vetted by a third-party verifier (see Resources) instead.

As an added bonus, switching over to more natural cleaning products means you'll no longer have to contend with that cloying, chemical smell of toxic home cleaners. And if you like that, here's a tip to take things that extra step forward: to make sure your domestic smells as fresh as your all-natural cleaning products, start adding house plants to every nook and cranny. Not only do they smell nice, they absorb toxins and clean your air!

If you're particularly partial to nice smells, consider investing in an essential oil diffuser. You can select any scent from peppermint to ylang ylang to set the mood. Say goodbye to synthetic, plug-in air fresheners made of plastic!

Goodbye Plastic
Personal Challenge

What one thing can I commit to that will reduce my use of plastic in the laundry room?

Pick a few changes to make to your routine and set a timeline for implementation. So as not to get overwhelmed, consider focusing on either the laundry room, bathroom or kitchen as a starting point as your first step and move onto the other rooms once you're done.

Citizen Activist Action

Make a donation to a non-profit that publishes guides ranking cleaning and laundry products. These third-party verifiers of products help keep manufacturers "honest" and provide the public with the information that enables us to pick the healthiest products for people and our planet.

Travel

Once you set off on a journey, whether to the airport or down the open road, a lot of things are out of your control. Plastic waste may seem like one of them, but it doesn't need to be.

For me, travelling light isn't just about how small my suitcase is. It's about keeping my plastic footprint as minimal as I can. This takes planning ahead, especially if you're travelling to countries like India where I visit our manufacturing partners regularly. Throw in road trips to visit friends in Southern California and to Death Valley and other natural monuments, and it becomes clear that it takes different tricks for different trips.

I take a modified version of my plastic-free toolkit with me wherever I travel; it reduces my plastic waste greatly. I'll share a simple approach to assembling a mini set of reusable items as well as other well-honed plastic-free travel tips to help you say no to single-use plastics on the go.

My Tiny To-Go Kit

Start by finding an unbreakable plastic-free container with about a six-cup capacity.

This works perfectly as the carrier for all of your plastic-free travel essentials and will keep you organized.

Next; water bottles. Bring two: one for hot drinks and one for cold. An insulated stainless steel container works well for hot beverages and a collapsible silicone bottle is great for water so you can keep weight and bulk down. For trips abroad, bring a filtration straw for when tap water isn't safe to drink.

Find a utensil or two that will fit inside the container you've selected. A small fork and spoon are good choices. I don't typically carry a knife since it won't clear airport security. You can purchase a foldable steel spork or find something small in your kitchen drawer or thrift shop.

If you like thick smoothies, a straw helps. For thick drinks, biodegradable straws usually won't work; they disintegrate too quickly. There are some good foldable straw options either made from steel and silicon or all silicon. I've found I like to pack a short glass straw with a cleaning brush. It's easy to see if it's clean after use since glass is see-through.

Last, find a reusable snack sack made from silicone, upcycled plastic polyester, or organic cotton that can be folded up to fit inside your container. Snack sacks are great for leftover sandwiches, baked goods, street foods, and other snacks that aren't too wet. Top everything off with a reusable cotton napkin to use as a placemat when eating in public places or to wipe up messes.

Plastic-Free Toiletries

Stock up on small reusable containers made from glass or metal to hold your lotions, creams, and toothpaste. Tiny glass jam jars and empty Altoids tins are great for this.

Another alternative is to use bar shampoos, conditioners, and deodorants. You can cut them down with a serrated knife to fit into any travel container. To keep your bar from creating a mess in your bag, try wrapping it in parchment paper, tin foil or reusable beeswax wrap. See the Kitchen chapter for several more saran-wrap swap suggestions.

Tote It Up

Bringing your own bag is an easy solution no matter where you travel.

Invariably, you'll pick up a souvenir or two from a trip. To prepare, find a compact reusable shopping bag and keep it with you everywhere you go. Clip it to the outside of your backpack, carry-on, or purse. Micro bags made from recycled plastic polyester that fold down to the size of an egg and hold more than 20 pounds are great for this. Some made from recycled cotton are a little bulkier but another great choice.

Food While Flying

Airports can be a real bear when it comes to plastic and, frankly, unless you pack all your own food with you it's nearly impossible to avoid. I'll share what I do to keep my plastic footprint as small as possible and not beat myself up about the stressful overload of plastic that comes my way while flying.

First off, use your reusable water bottle both in the airport (after you get through security) as well as on the aircraft. Flight attendants will happily pour water directly into your reusable water bottle.

To avoid buying heavily pre-packaged airport food, either bring your own homemade foods in reusable containers or buy food at an airport restaurant, not a kiosk where everything is in plastic tubs, and ask them to pack it in your reusable containers. On your first flight departing from home bringing your own food is manageable, but once you're in transit, you'll have to think ahead to strategize how to refuse unnecessary plastic. Do the best you can, but don't beat yourself up. Saying goodbye to plastic while travelling is a difficult maneuver.

Eco-Friendly Accommodations

You have many choices when it comes to travel accommodations. Choosing one that recognizes the importance of sustainability has become easier in recent years as more hotels embrace responsible tourism practices. From eliminating plastic straws and bottles to using solar power, the industry is shifting to create the sustainable travel experience that customers demand. Check hotel websites and call the front desk to vet them for alignment with your plastic-free values. Remember, to drive the market towards more sustainability, put your money where the plastic isn't.

Purification Made Easy

Have you ever considered purifying your water while traveling? It's easier than you think.

Purifying water on the go can be accomplished with filtration bottles, UV pens, and carbon-filled straws. I prefer using a pen or a straw to purify my water rather than bringing an all-in-one bottle system. Use a straw with an activated carbon capsule designed to remove bacteria, parasites, and microplastics and to reduce foul odors and tastes.

If you're looking for an all-in-one approach, consider a self-contained filtration and purification bottle. As a last resort, keep chlorine or iodine tablets on hand, but keep in mind that both have been linked to health issues and leave treated water with an unpleasant odor and taste. Sodium dichloroisocyanurate (NaDCC) is one alternative that achieves the same purifying results as chlorine with fewer risks.

Pre-Packaged Drinks: A Last Resort

No matter how well you plan, you may end up needing to purchase a bottled drink. There are better and worse choices when it comes to choosing your single-use bottle.

Pick a container made of more easily recyclable materials like a can or a glass bottle. Another good choice is to buy beverages sold in bottles made from recycled plastics, thereby supporting demand for goods made from recyclables. The recycled plastic might look cloudy, but don't let this dissuade you. Having clear plastic is one of the reasons that companies aren't transitioning to entirely recycled plastic.

Counterintuitive as it may seem, it's best to avoid drinks in bottles made from plant-based plastics. The bottles might be labeled as biodegradable in a commercial composting facility but it's highly unlikely this will be their end fate.

Recycling and composting systems aren't in place for these supposedly biodegradable plastics, so your container will almost certainly end up in the trash. In this way, compostable plastics are worse than regular petroleum-based plastics.

Goodbye Plastic Personal Challenge

What one thing can I commit to that will reduce my use of plastic when traveling?

Example: I will carry a tiny to-go kit filled with reusable, plastic-free items wherever I go.

Citizen Activist Challenge

There is little need for disposable plastic water bottles in most travel destinations. The more you can ask restaurants, hotels, and tour operators to refill your reusable water bottle, the more those services will cater to demand—and the less single-use plastic will be used.

Conclusion: Then, Now & Forever

The whales foraged all around us. As a girl, I remember, whales were on the brink of extinction, yet here they were: a dozen Humpback whales gloriously feeding all around our boat, explosively blowing vertical columns of vapor, commanding our attention in every direction. Like a dream come true, whale tales and dorsal fins were flaring out of the water 360 degrees around me like a maritime tiara. I was with my parents and children on the deck of an ecotourism cruise ship near Glacier Bay National Park in Alaska witnessing nature's resilience and abundance first-hand.

My flagging hopes for reigning in the growing threat of plastic pollution rebounded. I was struck with the realization that if humanity had saved whales already once in my lifetime, we could do it again and solve the planetary plastic crisis contributing to their demise.

All summer back at home in California, we'd been getting hammered with dreadful news of dead whales washing up along our coasts. More than 50 whales washed up dead or dying on West Coast beaches during the spring of 2019. Only a fraction of dead whales end up beachside, so the true number of whale deaths could be over ten times as many. Necropsies typically showed their bellies full of plastic debris: bundles of rope, plastic cups, bags, gloves, packing straps, tubing, and netting. Half a world away, that's what scientists found inside a dead sperm whale that washed up on a remote Scottish beach. Measuring 46 feet long, weighing more than 20 tons, scientists extracted more than 220 pounds of global plastic waste from the dead whale's stomach.

"We are a remote island," a clean-up volunteer explained, "and this [plastic] is floating in the ocean from all parts of the world."

During my childhood, whales had been imperiled by commercial exploitation, but their fate had been turned around. Their reprise from extinction was largely because of the passionate efforts of marine conservationist Dr. Roger Payne, who discovered that whales sing. Payne recorded the complex songs male humpbacks sing underwater and released a bestseller album called Songs of the Humpback Whale in 1970, allowing the whales' voices to be heard globally for the first time. Payne's recording celebrated their eerie anthem, forging an emotional connection between these majestic marine beings and humanity. Through opening our hearts, he succeeded in galvanizing a wellspring of public support for banning whaling and saving them from extinction.

Payne described whales as "humanity's canary in a coal mine" and in a 1979 *National Geographic* article wrote that, "Pollution will soon replace the harpoon as the next mortal threat to whales and, ultimately, humanity."

That mortal threat is here now. Now is the time to hear the whales song again and let these majestic creatures inspire us once again to open our hearts to the possibility of saving our seas. The time to act is now. It's all hands on deck. Whether you start your plastic-free journey in the kitchen, bathroom, or any other area of your life, all efforts matter.

Maybe you want to bring attention to the plastic peril in a song, or a letter to the editor. The plastic tidal wave we're facing is cresting. This is no time for regrets, for recriminations. It's no time for false promises, reassurances that future generations will surely figure out a solution; that, if only we had more people, money, equipment, or time, we could make a difference.

Wherever you are, you *can* make a difference. Please join us *now* in solving this problem, today. Together, we can protect what we love.

LOVE,

SANDRA

In Gratitude

dedicate this book to my children, for inspiring me to get personal with plastic pollution. Thank you for supporting me in my quest to make a lasting, positive difference in our world for generations to come. Thank you Nikolo and Mabel, for joining me in living as plastic-free as possible. I love you both and without you none of this would have been possible.

Thank you to my husband Thinh, for being my rock, my support crew: always ready to feed, drive, load, set up, test, tech support, and love me.

To my parents, I am forever grateful for your unwavering support and boundless curiosity about my work. I'm beholden as well to my grandparents and ancestors for standing steadfastly with me on this journey. You've built me from the ground up to be confident, to love our Earth, to believe I could make a difference. I am who I am thanks to you.

Along the way, I've needed a lot of advice from trusted advisors like Tara, Sharon, Paul, Steve, Jack and so many more that I can't name them all. Too often, I've also turned for help and moral support to my friends, those like Shalini, Andrea, Cynthia, Suzan, Karen, David and so many more confidantes who have shared such stretches of my plastic-free journey that I can't name them all here. Thank you to all of my advisors and friends for never laughing at my questions and always making yourselves available when I needed help (which was often)! Thank you, Dianna, for writing the foreword to this book and standing shoulder to shoulder with me to battle plastic pollution over the last decade. Knowing you are all there, along with the other warriors of the plastic-pollution movement, gives me hope and power to build a better future.

Bringing ECOlunchbox products to life wouldn't have happened without the trust and support of my longtime cherished business partners—Jignesh and Patrick—and their families. We did this together. I treasure our partnership and our friendship. I'm also so appreciative of the team of eco professionals powering ECOlunchbox's success from behind the scenes all these years. To all of you, thank you for believing in the potential of ECOlunchbox to empower people globally with our exceptionally made, plastic-free products.

The business of ECOlunchbox has been the greatest personal and professional development course one could ask for. Thank you, ECOlunchbox, for giving me a vessel to demonstrate love in action for my planet and for my children, showing the power of activating around one's values to make the world a better place.

And last but not least, thank you to the ECOlunchbox user community for using the power of your pocketbook to buy hundreds of thousands of our plastic-free food containers and put them to use. By believing in ECOlunchbox, you've averted the use and disposal of tens of millions of pieces of plastic trash every year, saving our oceans from needless plastic pollution.

Together, all of us—including those named here and those I've forgotten to recognize—have made a difference, and for this I am eternally grateful.

With love,

Sandra

Resources

The Plastic Pollution Crisis

Interested to learn more about the research and science of plastic pollution in our oceans? The Websites of 5 Gyres (www.5gyres.org), Algalita (algalita.org) and Lonely Whale (www.lonelywhale.org) offer many educational resources about plastic pollution and solutions.

Start tracking and recording plastic litter you find using Litterati. Using crowdsourcing and geotagging, the app creates litter maps and empowers governments and NGOs to organize cleanups and develop better policies around waste management. Download it for Apple or Android: www.litterati.org.

Listen to the emotive album Songs of The Humpback Whale to viscerally connect with these magnificent mammals and the sounds of our beloved Big Blue. Make sure the yellow and blue album cover specifies in the subtitle that the album is "The Original Classic Album of Whale Recordings Produced by Dr. Roger Payne." You can find it on most streaming music services like Spotify and Pandora: www.spotify.com and www.pandora.com.

Whale Alert is a free app for Apple devices allowing concerned citizens to report any sightings of live, dead, or distressed whales. It also provides known areas where whales migrate so captains can be more vigilant and try to avoid colliding with the mammals: www.whalealert.org.

World Oceans Day is a non-profit organization that organizes clean-ups. To find a beach clean-up near you, check out their event listings: www.worldoceansday.org. Cleaning up litter washed ashore can have a significant positive impact on our oceans. Removing it before it breaks down to microplastic particulate matter is a gift to our planet. You can find local beach clean-ups on Surfrider's crowd-sourced platform: cleanups.surfrider.org.

Second-Hand and Free Neighborhood Bulletin Boards

To reduce needless purchases, consider joining a gift economy community through the Buy Nothing Project, which operates volunteer groups globally using Facebook. To learn more, go to buynothingproject.org.

NextDoor is an online neighborhood bulletin board that's a good spot to post stuff you'd like to rehome. You're also welcome to use the app to ask for items you need, turning someone else's trash into your treasure. To sign up in your community, go to nextdoor.com.

To pick up second-hand utensils and place settings for plastic-free gatherings, check out Craigslist: www.craigslist.org/about/sites.

Fix It, Don't Ditch It

Broken bed, dresser, appliance, whatever? Don't ditch it, fix it! That's the motto of the Fixit Clinic, a volunteer organization that helps people learn how to fix their broken things instead of discarding them. Start a clinic or join one near you: fixitclinic.blogspot.com.

Bulk is Best

To find local grocery stores that sell in bulk, download the Zero Waste Home directory app: app.zerowastehome.com.

Similarly, to locate a food co-op where bulk foods are often sold by weight, visit these directory listings and search by state: coopdirectory.org or www.litterless.com/wheretoshop.

No More Junk Mail

To opt-out of unwanted mailing lists, go to the following website and provide your address: www.DirectMail.com/mail_preference and www.CatalogChoice.org. To stop receiving phone books, go to www.YellowPagesOptOut.com.

Eco Wardrobe Buying and Trading

To find thrift stores to buy from or donate clothing to, check out this online directory organized by state and sorted by zip code: www.thethrift shopper.com/zips.

You can also find meet-ups to swap clothes you no longer want or need. No cash exchanged, just clothes: www.meetup.com/topics/clothesswap.

Clean Products Guide

To learn about the chemicals and potential toxins that everyday consumer products contain check out reviews by the Environmental Working Group. The group publishes consumer guides on many topics, including cleaning products, cosmetics, and packaged foods here: www.ewg.org/consumer-guides.

Tap Water Refill Stations

Find drinking fountains and bottle refilling stations to top off your water bottle using the Tap website and app: tapitwater.com.

Bibliography

An SOS to the World

1. www.nationalgeographic.org/encyclopedia/great-pacific-garbage-patch/
2. Ellen MacArthur Foundation, The New Plastic Economy (2015)
3. www.researchgate.net/project/2016-17-South-Pacific-Expedition-en-route-to-the-Galapagos
4. Ellen MacArthur Foundation, The New Plastic Economy (2015)
5. ourworldindata.org/plastic-pollution

Kitchen & Shopping

1. blogs.ei.columbia.edu/2017/12/13/the-truth-about-bioplastics/
2. www.health.harvard.edu/staying-healthy/is-plastic-a-threat-to-your-health

3. www.statista.com/statistics/275956/us-house
   holds-quantity-of-rolls-of-plastic-wrap-used-
   within-6-months/
4. toxtown.nlm.nih.gov/chemicals-and-
   contaminants/perfluorooctanoic-acid-pfoa

Dining Room & Entertaining
1. oceanservice.noaa.gov/facts/pbde.html

Laundry Room & Cleaning
1. www.epa.gov/facts-and-figures-about-
   materials-waste-and-recycling/textiles-material-
   specific-data

Index
